The Second Course of Orthographic Projection

THE SECOND COURSE

OF

ORTHOGRAPHIC PROJECTION;

BEING A CONTINUATION OF

THE NEW METHOD OF TEACHING THE SCIENCE

OF

MECHANICAL AND ENGINEERING DRAWING;

WITH SOME PRACTICAL REMARKS

ON

THE TEETH OF WHEELS,

THE PROJECTION OF SHADOWS, PRINCIPLES OF SHADING, AND DRAWING FROM

MACHINERY.

INTENDED FOR THE INSTRUCTION OF ENGINEERS, ARCHITECTS, BUILDERS,
MASONS, &c., AND FOR THE USE OF SCIENCE SCHOOLS AND CLASSES.

WITH   NUMEROUS   ILLUSTRATIONS.

BY

WILLIAM BINNS,

CONSULTING ENGINEER, ASSOC. INST. C.E.,

LATE MASTER OF THE MECHANICAL DRAWING CLASS AT THE DEPARTMENT OF SCIENCE
AND ART, AND AT THE ROYAL SCHOOL OF MINES; FORMERLY
PROFESSOR OF APPLIED MECHANICS
AT THE COLLEGE FOR CIVIL ENGINEERS, ETC., ETC., ETC.

LONDON:

E. & F. N. SPON, 48, CHARING CROSS.

1869.

LONDON :
KELLY AND CO., PRINTERS,
GATE STREET, LINCOLN'S INN FIELDS, W.C.

PREFACE.

In the preface to the first edition of my Elementary Treatise on Orthographic Projection, and its application to Mechanical and Engineering Drawing, it is stated that a Second Course may hereafter form the subject of another treatise, embracing the "delineation of worm, bevel, mitre, and spur wheels; the principles of the formation of the teeth of wheels, and the practical modes of constructing them by means of templets and the 'Odontograph'; the cycloid, epicycloid and hypocycloidal curves; the construction of cams, wipers, heart-wheels, and eccentrics; the projection of shadows; and the practice of making to scale drawings from actual machinery." *

Circumstances, however, to which it will be unnecessary, if not painful, to advert, led me for some years to abandon the idea of writing the second part of a book which men who have had no practice in the workshop have so pertinaciously tried to put down; but I have from time to time

---

* As many of the problems in this " Second Course" are required to be worked out to a given scale, I beg to refer those students who are not acquainted with the Engineer's Scale to ART. 217, p. 177.

been aroused to the importance of the subject by
the receipt of letters the tone and purport of which
may be gathered from the following extract:—

" Sir,—   " South Devon, 6/1/1869.

    *   *   *   *   *

" Is it taking too great a liberty to request you to inform me
when the demand for this work may be met. Like many others,
I have studied (and may say roughly mastered) your Elementary
Treatise; and such great interest has it given me that, having
passed the 2nd grade, S. K. examination in Mechanical
Drawing, I want now to pursue the study for my own pleasure.
Being unwilling, however, to wait indefinitely, I have taken the
liberty of applying to you for information as to when the long
wished for continuation of your first *invaluable* treatise may be
placed in our hands. If I and my fellow-students have still to
wait some months longer, might I venture to ask you what book
on the subject (and where obtainable) you could recommend
for study meantime. I feel I owe you a thousand apologies for
the liberty I have taken in thus addressing you, but, presuming
upon the love of inducing progress in young aspirants evinced
by the publication of your deservedly appreciated treatise, I
have hoped you will excuse it from one who tenders you sincere
thanks for having opened to students so delightful and profitable
a source of instruction.

             " I beg to remain, Sir,
                 " Yours respectfully,
" To Wm. Binns, Esq."   " C. B———.

My best thanks are eminently due to those
gentlemen who have encouraged me to prepare
this Second Course of Orthographic Projection,
and its application to Mechanical and Engineering
Drawing, in which I have endeavoured to give a
resumé of a course of lectures delivered by me at
the late College for Civil Engineers, Putney, and

also at the Department of Science and Art, South Kensington. There will also be found much additional matter relating to the importance of establishing a uniform system for the formation of the teeth of wheels and the mode of carrying the same into effect. I beg, especially, to call the attention of Engineers and Pattern Makers to that part of my work which treats on this subject, in the hope that the anomalous practice which still exists in this important branch of mechanical engineering may soon be changed.

I have to thank my esteemed friend, Mr. William Rye, the Mayor of Oldham—Messrs. Robert Wood and Sons, of Leeds—Messrs. Ormrod, Grierson, and Co., of Manchester—Messrs. Robinson, Cooks, and Co., of St. Helen's, Lancashire, and other eminent men who have kindly furnished me with details of the various methods now in use for describing the teeth of wheels, from which I have, without materially altering that form which is acknowledged to be the best, endeavoured to introduce a form of tooth that shall be UNIVERSAL.

WILLIAM BINNS.

LAKE, SANDOWN,
    ISLE OF WIGHT,
        1st November, 1869.

CONTENTS.

CHAPTER VII.

The Delineation of Spur Wheels.

CHAPTER VIII.

Mortise and other Wheels.

CHAPTER IX.

Teeth of Wheels in Practice.

CHAPTER XIII.

The Projections of Shadows.

CHAPTER XIV.

Shading and Colours.

CHAPTER XV.

Drawing from the Machine and Copying Drawings.

ORTHOGRAPHIC PROJECTION.

before proceeding with this Second Course of Orthographic Projection and its application to Mechanical and Engineering Drawing, to guard him against those things which are likely to cause annoyance by interfering with his success. For instance, he may have noticed, when attempting to draw a fine and solid line, that the pen will work remarkably well on almost any part of the paper except that part where the line is required. He may also have observed, when drawing a long fine line, that the ink will cease to flow from the pen before the line is finished; or that the line when finished is solid, but not

B

of uniform thickness; or it may be that the line when drawn is broken up, or unsound—commonly called a "rotten line." It will, therefore, be our first duty to explain the circumstances that tend to produce those defects in outlines which are traceable to one or more of the following causes—viz., the pen, the paper, the ink, or a want of proper care on the part of the draughtsman.

ART. 1.—*Drawing Pen.*—This instrument is used for drawing straight and curved lines with the assistance of a straight-edge or a "French curve." The pen in general use consists of two steel blades, or "nibs," secured, by brazing, to a brass stock, which is usually attached to a bone or ivory handle; the "nibs," being so formed as to spring open, are adjustable by a milled-headed screw to draw lines of any degree of fineness. There is another form of pen, in which one of the nibs is attached to the stock by a hinge joint, with a steel spring between the two blades to force them apart: this form, however, is not so good as the one just described.

Now, the two nibs, or point, of a drawing pen must be very accurately ground or *set;* and as this operation of *setting* is one that requires frequent repetition and some practice, the following instructions may possibly be of service.

In the first place, the nibs must be precisely of the same length, rounded in two directions, and as sharp as it is possible to make them without producing to the touch a sensation of cutting, and without scratching the surface of the paper when drawing a line, which is generally the case when one nib is longer than the other. This irregularity may be detected by placing, alternately, the sides of the pen at an acute angle to the fore-finger and slipping the edge of the nail over the point, when the difference in length will be at once perceived; and it may be reduced by drawing a few lines, as it were, on a Turkey stone, with the pen applied to the edge of a set square in the

same manner as if drawing lines upon paper, but with
this difference, that during the longitudinal motion of the
pen the handle must be turned over in a circular manner,
so as to give a rounded form to the point of the pen. If
the pen be now held with the point directed towards the
eye, and gently moved about so as to catch the angle of
of reflection, a bright speck on one or both nibs will be
observed, which must be reduced by rubbing the pen to
and fro upon the stone, giving at the same time a slight
rotary motion to the handle, which must be held at an
angle of about 20° with the face of the stone; the point
of the pen being examined from time to time, and the
process of reducing the bright specks continued until the
point is as fine as can be used without cutting or scratching
the paper.

If at this stage the two nibs are of the same length, a
perfectly solid and fine line can be drawn. The beginner,
however, must not be disappointed if sixty minutes are
thus expended before he can produce a satisfactory result;
whereas two minutes in the hands of a practitioner would
suffice.

It may have been noticed when drawing a long and
fine line with the pen in perfect order, that the line is
not throughout of the same thickness. This disagreeable
result arises in most cases from an unequal pressure of
the pen against the edge of the **T** square, thus causing a
deflection of the back nib, and interfering with the flow
of ink, which cannot be uniform if the pressure is unequal,
and the line is consequently uneven.

This deflection, and the amount of pressure that will
cause it, may be practically illustrated by charging the
pen with ink and pressing the back nib against the edge
of the finger nail, when the surface of the ink will be
seen to rise slightly between the nibs, the pen being held
in a vertical position.

ART. 2.—*Paper*.—The well-known material on which
mechanical and engineering drawings are made is pre-

pared in sheets, the names and dimensions of which are as follow :—   *Inches.*

Antiquarian .	.	.	53	×	31
Atlas	.	. .	34	×	26
Columbier	.	.	34½	×	23½
Demy	.	. .	20	×	15
Double Elephant .	.	40	×	26¾
Elephant .	.	. .	28	×	23
Emperor	.	.	68	×	48
Imperial .	.	. .	30	×	22
Royal .	.	. .	24	×	19¼
Super Royal	.	. .	27½	×	19¼

There are many other sizes of papers, but the imperial, elephant, and double elephant are most in use for drawing purposes, and may be had with a glazed or plain surface, the latter with a fine open texture being generally preferred. Some draughtsmen, however, prefer to use glazed paper for outline drawings, and unglazed paper for colored drawings.

ART. 3.—*Straining Paper on the Drawing Board.*—This operation is variously performed, each draughtsman adopting his peculiar way, and with varied success. The writer prefers the following plan :—Some melted glue and a small glue brush being provided, the sheet to be strained is laid face upwards on the drawing board. A wet sponge is then passed rapidly along the margins (that is, round the sheet), and then across the sheet, including margins, until the whole surface is well wetted. The object of wetting the margins first is to prevent cockling, by giving those parts a little longer time for expansion than the middle of the sheet, which may now be left for about ten minutes before glueing down on the board. The process of glueing should be commenced along *one end* of the sheet; for this purpose a straight edge is laid across the end, and a quarter of an inch of the margin turned up against it and glued; the glued part is then laid flat, and rubbed down with the handle of a knife or tooth brush. The opposite end of the sheet must then be treated in the same way, and pulled outwards; and after that, the top and bottom margins must be glued down in like manner, and the board left in a horizontal position until the paper, which ought to be protected from dust, is quite dry; for, if the board be immediately turned on edge, the water will gravitate and soften the glue on the lower margin, which will leave the board, and in that case be very troublesome to repair. This will also be the result if the board be placed near a fire for the purpose of drying the paper.

Art. 4.—*Indian Ink.*—This is prepared for use by rubbing with water in one of a nest of saucers, for which there should be a good fitting cover. The saucer ought to be quite smooth inside, so as not to abrade the ink, which, when mixed to the required blackness, should immediately be covered, to protect it from such particles of dust as are constantly floating about a room.

In order to supply the pen with ink, it will be necessary in the first instance to moisten the nibs by placing them between the lips, or by other means, when, if the point of the pen be placed in the ink, the fluid will rise, by capillary attraction, between the nibs: the ink adhering to the exterior parts of the pen must be removed by drawing them over a piece of blotting paper. This method of filling the pen with ink will be found much cleaner and more convenient than supplying the ink with a brush.

Notwithstanding every care on the part of the draughtsman, particles of dust settling on the sheet of paper will be taken up by and mixed with the ink in the pen, and, assisted by the evaporation of the fluid mixture, will cause the pen to be clogged up. When this takes place, the obstruction must be removed by drawing between the nibs a slip of writing paper, and not by slackening the screw, which, being once set for fine lines, should not be altered, except in cases where the pen requires *setting*. For thick or shadow lines another pen should always be employed.

ART. 5.—*Renewing the Ink.*—Indian ink, after it has become thick or dried up, may be renewed as follows:— Let the draughtsman keep at hand a piece of india-rubber about the size and shape of two joints of the forefinger of the hand. When the ink is dried up in the saucer, but not in flakes, it may be reduced to an impalpable paste by grinding it with the india-rubber, the end whereof has been previously wetted; a drop of water being added from time to time as the rubbing proceeds: this operation improves the quality of the ink, by reducing the gritty particles. The water must not be allowed to drop into the saucer at the commencement of the operation, as that might cause the ink to leave the saucer in flakes, which would have to be removed and the saucer washed out. In order to reduce the amount of evaporation when the ink is not in use, the writer places a ring of vulcanized india-rubber over the *lip* or rim of the saucer and weights the cover (*which must be replaced every time after a supply of ink has been taken*) with lead: in this manner ink may be kept in good working order for several weeks, care being taken to remove the *flakes,* should any appear, before using the india-rubber. Precipitation or thickening must be corrected by the addition of water and a few rubs with the "rubber" or indian ink, as the case may require.

ART. 6.—*Precautionary Remarks.*— Although the hands of the draughtsman may, and at all times ought to be, scrupulously clean, there will always be an amount of insensible perspiration, the deposit of which on the surface of the paper will account for the pen making a better line on one part of the sheet than on another part; consequently, the hands, when not supported by the **T** square, should rest upon a loose piece of paper kept for the purpose; if these instructions are followed there will be no difficulty in drawing a fine solid line when and where required.

ART. 7.—*Joining Right and Curved Lines.*—It is much easier to join a right line to a circular arc than it is to join a circular arc to a right line; therefore, when inking-in a

drawing, all the circles and arcs of circles should be put
in before commencing with the right lines. When arcs
of circles have to be joined to arcs of other circles, or a
right line to an arc, it is necessary, before inking-in, to
determine the point or points at which the arcs should
meet each other, or the arc meet the right line; for if two
such lines have to meet, and one of them be carried
beyond its proper limit, a defect in that part of the curve
will be the result. The mode of defining the point at
which two lines ought to meet will be understood from
the following explanation:—

Let *a b c* in the accompanying diagram, Fig. 1, represent a compound curved line, and *c d* a right line joined
thereto. If such a combination of
lines were sketched in pencil, and it
were required to put them in ink,
the first thing would be to find, by
trial, the centres *e* and *f* of the two
curves *a b, b c*; now, if *e* and *f* be
joined by a right line, the point of

Fig. 1.

intersection *b* will be that at which *a b* and *c b* must
meet; furthermore, the point *c*, where the curve *b c*
joins the right line *c d*, is determined by drawing
from *f* a line perpendicular to *c d*: therefore *b* and *c* are
the points at which the lines must meet. Again, the
common intersection of the compound curve *s p r* in *p* is
determined by drawing a right line through the centres
n o, from which the curves are drawn.

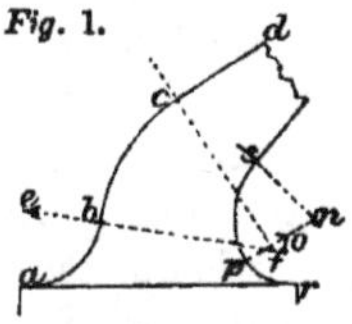

CHAPTER II.

EXAMPLES IN PRACTICE.

IN a popular work on Mechanical and Engineering Drawing, it is stated that " the delineation of a screw of several threads does not possess any additional point of difficulty " over the projection of a screw with a single thread, and the student is left without an attempt being made to give him any further knowledge of the subject. But the writer of the present treatise has found the projection of a square-top-and-bottom three-threaded screw to present difficulties to many students, who have been puzzled to get in the required number of threads; for this reason, and also as it is intended to show the application of the principle of the projection of helices to the projection of other objects, it is deemed necessary to enter fully into the mode of finding the projection of a three-threaded screw, which was only briefly alluded to in the Elementary Treatise.

In all cases it is recommended that the student should test his knowledge of projection, by trying to work out the problem before reading the explanation.

PROBLEM I.

Given the diameter and pitch of a screw with three square-top-and-bottom threads, to find the vertical projection thereof.

ART. 8.—Dimensions of the screw to be as follow :—

Diameter at the top of thread   . . $2\frac{3}{8}$ inches.
Diameter at the bottom of thread   . $1\frac{13}{16}$ inch.
Pitch of thread   .   .   . $1\frac{1}{4}$ inch.

On the base or intersecting line I L, No. 1, Drawing A, describe a semicircle 0 2 4, equal in diameter
to the diameter of the screw at the top of the thread; and
divide the semicircle into any number of equal parts
(say four) in points 1, 2, 3, from which draw the radii
1 5, 2 5, 3 5. From points 0, 1, 2, 3, 4, draw lines 0 0', 1 1', 2 2',
&c., perpendicular to I L, which will represent the vertical
projection of the meridians. Upon any given line A B,
drawn parallel to the lines just described, set off A c, equal
to the pitch of the screw; divide A c into six equal parts
(that is, into *twice the number of parts that there are threads
in the screw*), and continue the divisions along the line
A B for any given length of screw, observing that each
division or part represents a thread or a space: for a
three-threaded screw there are three threads and three
spaces or intervals within the pitch; and this rule applies
to any other number of threads. Upon a loose slip of
paper, as represented by *e f g h*, draw a right line *i k*;
set off *k l*, equal to the pitch of the screw; and divide
k l very accurately into eight equal parts, which, being
twice the number of parts contained in the semicircle,
will represent one convolution of the helix, as indicated
by the dotted line *m* 4'. If the loose slip of paper be now
applied to the foregoing construction, with the line *i k*
parallel to the axis of the screw, the projections of three
of the large curves, commencing at the points *m, n, o*, can
be obtained, as shown by the construction lines. When
the projections of the curves *m m'*, *n n'*, and *o* 4' have
been found, move the slip of paper so that one of the divisions will correspond with a horizontal line drawn from the
point *p*, and proceed to find that and the remaining large
curves in like manner. The loose slip of paper greatly
facilitates and simplifies the operation, which would otherwise require several lines to be divided similar to *i k* and
a multiplication of points, which would be embarrassing
to the student. The curves representing the bottom of the
thread or its intersection with the cylinder are obtained

in like manner; that is, by describing a semicircle *r s t*, to represent the depth of the thread (which is generally made equal to the interval or space between the threads), and drawing perpendicular lines from its points of intersection with the radial lines, and horizontal lines from the points on line *k l*, as described for the projection of the large curves.

No. 2 represents a vertical section of a nut for the above screw; the mode of projecting which is the same as for the thread of the screw, the inclination of the curves being reversed. (See ART. 168, Elem. Treat.)

ART. 9.—It may be observed that the first curve of a screw or other similar object having been found, by projecting the points as described, the remaining curves could be obtained by setting off with a pair of dividers a number of points, representing the threads and intervals, along the vertical lines 1 1′, 2 2′, &c.; but for a good outline drawing this plan will not do, because the points of the compasses would deface the paper, and the small punctures would interfere with the flow of ink from the pen; consequently all the points should be projected and carefully drawn in pencil. When "inking-in" the drawing, it will be of advantage to find centres for those portions of the curves at *n, n′, m*, &c., as they can be put in with a bow-pen; and the remaining portions of the helix can be drawn with the aid of a "French curve," of which there are a great variety of forms, but the one most generally useful is shown in the accompanying wood-cut, Fig. 2:

Fig. 2.

they are from 10 to 12 inches long, and will be found to answer every purpose required by the mechanical engineer's draughtsman.

HELICAL SPRINGS.

PROBLEM II.

*Required the vertical projection of a helical spring, made
from a piece of steel one quarter of an inch thick and
half an inch wide, the diameter of spring being two inches
and a quarter, and the pitch seven-eighths of an inch.*

ART. 10.—Upon I L, the intersecting line of No. 1,
Drawing B, describe a semicircle o 2 4, of the required
diameter of the spring; divide the semicircle into four
equal parts, and erect perpendiculars, as hereinbefore
explained. With a loose slip of paper *e f g h*, on which
the pitch of the spring, subdivided into eight equal
parts, has been accurately set off and continued along the
line *i k*, find the projections of the long curves o 1', 3 3', 5 5'.
Upon the vertical line drawn from point o, set off o 2, equal
to the thickness of the piece of steel of which the spring
is made; then move the slip of paper *e f g h*, so that one of
the divisions will coincide with a horizontal line drawn
from point 2, and proceed to find the projections of the
long curves, commencing at points 2, 4, and 6. Having
carefully pencilled in the curves representing the anterior
portion of the spring, find the projection of the return
curves, commencing at 2', 4', 6', 5, and 3: about two-thirds
only of the length of each curve will be required. From
o set off o' equal to the breadth of the steel of which the
spring is supposed to be made, and describe the semicircle
o' 2' 4'. The projections of the short curves representing
the inner convolutions of the spring will be readily understood from the construction lines, observing that the
termination of each curve is on the centre line, which
indicates the axis of the helix.

ART. 11.—The projection of a helical spring made from
a cylindrical piece of steel, or the projection of a worm
such as is used for distillation, is exhibited at No. 2,

Drawing B, and from what has already been said, will require but little explanation. Having laid down a plan of the helical spring or worm, as shown by *a b c*, set off upon a line *e f*, drawn parallel to the axis, the height of each convolution or pitch of the helix, and proceed, as before described, to find the vertical projection of the centre line *a* 3 4. With a radius equal to that of the pipe or piece of steel (as the case may be), and from those points in the meridians which are intersected by the helix, describe a number of circles, and proceed to draw in the lines representing the upper and lower surfaces of the coil; which lines will be tangential to the small circles representing the diameter of the pipe or piece of steel; care being taken not to extend the lines beyond the tangential point of the circles at *o, o*.

Art. 12.—In cases where less accuracy is required, the several coils or convolutions may· be projected in right lines drawn tangentially to semicircles, as shown at No. 3, Drawing B, which represents the ordinary mode of delineating a helical spring.

In workshop phraseology springs of the above form are commonly, but somewhat erroneously, called spiral springs; the term helix amongst practical engineers is but seldom heard, notwithstanding it would appear to be required, if only to mark the difference betwixt a spring, or worm, when made in the form of a cylinder, and when made in the form of a cone. The misapplication of the term spiral does not, however, stop here, for it is also made to include another form of spring. See " The Imperial Dictionary," in which the first definition of spiral is " winding round a fixed point or centre, and continually receding from it, like a watch-spring." The same writer,[*] however, in his admirable work, gives the following definition of spiral, as applied to *architecture* and *sculpture:* " A curve that ascends winding about a cone or spire, so that

---

* John Ogilvie, LL.D.

every point of it continually approaches the axis. It is
thus distinguished from the helix or screw, which winds
in the same manner about a cylinder." If the reader will
accept the first of these definitions as describing a *convolute
spring*, he will then be acquainted with the technical
names of the different forms of springs noticed in this
work.

SPIRAL SPRINGS.

ART. 13.—The mode of projecting this form of spring
will be understood on referring to No. 4, Drawing B.
Having determined upon its dimensions, and drawn in the
half plan, consisting of two concentric semicircles, find
the vertical projection of the frustum of the spire or cone
a b c d, and next find the meridians or vertical projections
of the lines 11′, 3 3′. From the line *e f*, upon which the
pitch of the spring has been set off, draw horizontal lines
to intersect the meridians, and proceed as already described
for the projection of the helical spring No. 2; or, if less
accuracy be required, as described (ART. 12) for No. 3.

ART. 14.—Springs of this kind, when made in the form
shown at No. 5, Drawing B (*i. e.*, two frustums united at
their smaller ends), are extensively used for spring cushions
and mattresses, as also for moderator lamps, on account
of their having a greater range of action than the cylindrical helix, which is due to the coils of the spring being
made to move within one another somewhat in the manner
of the tubes of a telescope. It may be observed that the
horizontal projection of a spiral spring would be a convolute in form; the object and action of the two springs
are, however, very dissimilar, the former being employed
to produce rectilinear force and motion, whilst the latter
produces circular motion, as in the case of watch-
springs.

CONVOLUTES OR SCROLLS.

ART. 15.—The geometrical mode of drawing a convolute spring, sometimes, but erroneously, called a spiral spring, is only practicable within certain limits; but in cases where not more than two or three convolutions are required, such as in scrolls for handrails, the following method will be found to produce very nearly a symmetrical curve.

PROBLEM III.

Let it be required to describe a scroll of any given number of convolutions between two given points in a radius.

ART. 16.—Upon a right line drawn from A, No. 6, Drawing B, the centre of the scroll, set off A B the largest radius, and A C equal to the smallest radius of the scroll. Divide B C into two equal parts, in point D, and divide C D or D B into equal parts, consisting of *one part more than the number of convolutions required in the scroll.* From A, the centre of the scroll, set off A e, A h, each equal to the half of one of those parts. Then will e h be equal to one-fourth of B D when three convolutions are required, and one-third of B D when two convolutions are required, and so on for any number of convolutions. From e and h, upon the line A B, construct the square f e h g; and from f and g draw lines f A, g A. Divide f A, g A, into as many equal parts as there are convolutions; and from each division in f A, g A, construct smaller squares, whose sides are parallel to f e, h g. Produce e f indefinitely to K, f g to L, and g h to M. From e as a centre, and with e B as radius, describe the quadrant B K; from f as a centre, with the radius f K, describe the quadrant K L; from g as a centre, with g L as radius, describe L M; and from h, with the radius h M, describe the quadrant M D, which will complete one convolution of the scroll. The second convolution is obtained in like manner from the corresponding angles or corners of the next square; and the third convolution in the same way from the smallest square.

No. 7 represents the plan of a scroll for a handrail with two convolutions.

STAIRS.

ART. 17.—From the knowledge which the student may be supposed to have acquired in working out .the foregoing problems, it will not be necessary to enter very minutely into the projection of stairs, notwithstanding the variety of forms which such structures assume, inasmuch as the principles already explained are applicable to every description of stairs. It is proposed, however, to give two or three examples for practice in delineation.

Having laid down a plan of the space that can be afforded for the reception of the stairs, commonly called the staircase, the next thing will be to set off the height of the floor, or ascent of the flight of stairs, and divide that distance into a certain number of equal parts, each part representing the rise of a step. The number of steps being set off on a vertical line, drawn parallel to the axis of the staircase, as a b, No. 1, Drawing C, we must then proceed to lay down in the plan the "treads," or breadth of each step, from c to d, commencing with the bottom step, when it will immediately be ascertained whether the space allowed for the stairs will admit of a half-space landing (as shown at No. 2), a quarter-space landing (as shown at No. 4), or whether "winders" will be required: the latter, it may be observed, are not the most convenient for carpets, and on that account it is desirable for stairs requiring such covering to adopt when practicable the half-space or quarter-space landing.

To obtain the vertical projection of the stairs, it is only necessary to erect perpendicular lines from the corner of each step in the plan, and draw horizontal lines from the corresponding points on the line *a b*, representing the rise of each step, as will be understood on referring to the construction lines of No. 1. The ornamental parts, such as the nosings and brackets on the string boards, may then be drawn in according to taste and the class of stairs required, as shown at No. 3, Drawing C.

ART. 18.—In ordinary houses the breadths of the steps are generally from 10 to 12 inches, the heights from 6 to $7\frac{1}{2}$ inches, and the lengths from 2 feet 6 inches to 4 feet. In more stately mansions the steps may be from 4 to 6 inches high, from 12 to 15 inches broad, and 6 feet long, and upwards in proportion thereto.

HANDRAILS.

ART. 19.—As the projection of the handrail over a circular plan cannot in all cases be regulated by geometrical principles, the student will find, on attempting the projection of a flight of stairs and handrail, such as that shown at No. 3, Drawing C, that the circular rise will produce a disagreeable line or deformity in the curve of the rail, which must be removed by what the joiner terms " easing " the rail, that is, giving a more regular and uniform sweep to the curve at those parts where it is joined by the right lines *l m, n o*, at the points *m* and *n*. The projection of handrails may, however, as a rule, be found on the principle laid down for the projection of helical curves in ART. 8, that is, by finding, as therein described, the projection of any number of imaginary lines on the surface of the rail.

ART. 20.—Notwithstanding the deformity spoken of, the above mode of finding the projection of a handrail is the best, and particularly for the rail of a circular stair-

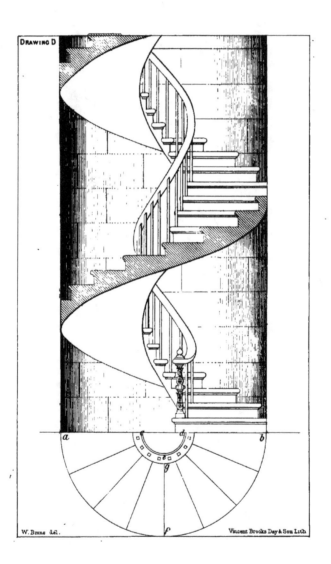

DRAWING D

W. Binns del.

Vincent Brooks Day & Son Lith

case, such as that shown on Drawing D, which is given as an exercise for the student to work out to scale as accurately as possible, say 1¼ inch to the foot, the dimensions of the staircase and stairs being as follow :—

	ft.	*in.*
Diameter of staircase, *a b* . . .	6	10
Diameter of " well-hole," or inner circle of hand-rail, *c d*	1	7
Rise of each step		6
Length of step, *e f*, exclusive of nosing .	2	7½
Breadth of hand-rail, *e g* . . .		3
Height of balusters, of which there should be one to each step . . .	2	4
Number of steps in the circular plan to be sixteen.		

The grandest example of this description of staircase upon a circular base may be seen in the clock-tower of St. Paul's cathedral.

SCREW PROPELLERS.

Before leaving the subject of the helix and spiral, it will be desirable to show the application of the principles already explained to the projection of some of the forms of screws which were originally designed for propelling vessels. Notwithstanding some of the examples given are almost useless for the purpose for which they were intended, the student will find them suitable objects for study and practice in delineation.

The first form of propeller we shall notice is one invented by Mr. Bennet Woodcroft, A.D 1832, and is remarkable only for having a gradually increasing pitch.

PROBLEM IV.

Required the projection of two revolutions of a helical screw with a gradually increasing pitch, showing the intersection of the blade with the screw shaft.

ART. 21.—The following are the dimensions :—

	ft.	*in.*
Diameter of screw at top of thread or blade	2	6
Pitch of first revolution . . .	2	0
Ditto of second revolution . . .	3	0
Diameter of shaft	0	4½

Scale ¾ inch to 1 foot.

This and the following problems on screw propellers are given in the form of an examination, in order that the student may test his knowledge of the principles of helical projections and their application to the arts, before reading the text or consulting the drawings. Should his efforts not be quite successful, the following brief description will remove all difficulty.

Draw the rectangle *a b c d*, No. 1, Drawing E, equal to the length and diameter of the screw, 5 feet × 2 feet 6 inches. Upon the centre line *e f* describe the semi-circle 1 3 4, and divide it in the manner hereinbefore described (ART. 8). From *b*, and at any given angle with *b c*, draw an indefinite right line *b g*; and set off from *b*, on the line *b g*, sixteen equal parts (which, as a matter of convenience, should not exceed in length the entire length of the screw). From *b*, on the line *b c*, set off *b h*, equal to the pitch of the first revolution of the screw = 2 feet; from *h* draw an indefinite right line through the eighth point or division on the line *b g*; and from *c*, another indefinite right line through the sixteenth point, cutting the line *h* 8, in some point *i*. If lines be now drawn from point *i*, through the equal divisions on the line *b g*, so as to intersect the line *b c*, the latter will be divided in such

manner that any two consecutive divisions will be in the
ratio of 3 to 2; and if the blade of the screw, and its intersection with the axis, be projected from points on the line
b c, and the meridian lines 1, 2, 3, as described for the
thread of a screw, the result will be the projection of a
screw propeller with a gradually increasing pitch.

Problem V.

*Required the projection of the end and side elevations of a
screw propeller of an elliptical form, with four threads or
blades, showing the intersection of the blades with the axis.*

Art. 22.—The dimensions of propeller are as follow:

	ft.	in.
Major axis of ellipse	7	10½
Minor axis of ellipse	3	9
Pitch of each blade	5	3
Diameter of propeller shaft . . .	0	8½

Scale ½ inch to 1 foot.

Upon a centre line, as *a b*, No. 2, Drawing E, describe
(in the manner directed by Art. 122 of the Elem. Treat.)
an ellipse, whose major axis=7 feet 10½ inches, and minor
axis = 3 feet 9 inches. Perpendicular to *a b* draw *c d*;
and from *a*, the point of intersection of the two lines *a b*
and *c d*, describe a semi-circle, equal in diameter to the
minor axis of the ellipse, which may be divided, as hereinbefore described, into four equal parts by meridian lines
a 1, *a* 2, &c. From the vertex of the ellipse, and perpendicular to *a b*, draw *e f*; and from any point in *e f*, draw
e g, parallel to *a b*, making *e g* equal to the pitch of one of
the blades=5 feet 3 inches. Divide *e g* into eight equal
parts 1′, 2′, 3′, &c.; and from each point let fall a perpendicular, or double ordinate to the ellipse. We must now
proceed to find the projections of the meridian lines *a* 1,

c 2

a 3, on the ellipse. For this purpose it will be sufficient to take any two or more ordinates as radii, say $i\,i'$, $k\,k'$, and from *a* as a centre, describe semi-circles i^2, k^2, intersecting the meridians *a* 1. *a* 3, in points *l* and *m*. From *l* and *m* draw lines parallel to *a b*, intersecting the ordinates $i\,i^1$, $k\,k^1$, in points *n, o, &c.*, for any number of points, through which the meridian *n o p*, shown by dotted lines, must be carefully drawn by hand, or with a French curve.

On the four blades and their intersection with the propeller shaft it will not be requisite to dwell, as the convolutions of the two blades, which commence on the upper and lower sides of the axis, are clearly shown by dotted and full lines, and their points of intersection with the double ordinates and meridian lines can be so distinctly traced, that a further description, for those who understand the projection of a common helix, is considered unnecessary.

No. 3, Drawing E, represents an end elevation of the propeller, with its four blades, which are obtained by describing a circle of the same diameter as the propeller shaft, and six concentric circles of the same diameter as the double ordinates, and drawing the curvilinear blades through the points of intersection of the meridian lines with the double ordinate circles. For instance, the upper curve or blade, commencing at f', will (for a right-hand screw) pass through the intersection of the first circle with the meridian line *a* 1, and through the intersection of the second circle with the line *a* 2, and so on to the sixth circle, which represents the greatest diameter of the propeller. This form of propeller was patented by Mr. Miles Berry in the year 1840.

ART. 23.—The next description of propeller to be given as an example in the projection of curvilinear figures is one that was invented in 1839 by the late Mr. George Rennie, and is designated a " revolving cone or conoid " with two threads or blades; the sides of the cone being concave. See No. 4, Drawing E.

Problem VI.

Let it be required to find the projection, comprising an elevation and plan or end view, of a conical propeller with two right-handed blades, and of the following dimensions:—

	ft.	in.
Diameter of cone at base	6	10
Height of cone or length of screw	5	0
Sides of cone to be concave and drawn with a radius of	5	8
Pitch of each blade	3	4
The propeller shaft or axis to be a perfect cone whose base =	0	7½
and height =	5	0

Scale ½ inch to 1 foot.

Note.—These figures are not given as the actual dimensions of the propellers, but simply as a guide for the student in the production of symmetrical objects for delineation.

If the student has not been quite successful in his endeavours to find the projection of the foregoing figure, he is recommended to make a careful study, on an enlarged scale, of No. 6, Drawing E, which will no doubt lead to a solution of the more difficult problem contained in Nos. 4 and 5.

Art. 24.—On referring to No. 6, which represents a left-handed screw of a spiral form, it will be seen that the plan consists of three semicircles, three radials, and a base line. The first semicircle represents the largest diameter of the axis; the second semicircle the upper end of the frustum *a b;* and the largest semicircle the horizontal projection of the base *c d.* Now the vertical projection of point 1 is *e*, and the vertical projection of point 2 is *f;* join *f e;* then will *e f* be the vertical projection of the radial line 1, 2. Having thus got the meridians upon the frustum and also upon the axis, all the curves will be found in the manner described for the projection of a common helix.

ART. 25.—With regard to Nos. 4 and 5, Drawing E, the first operation is to get the external form of the conoid; for this purpose draw two lines, *a b* and *c d*, at right angles to each other, and make them respectively equal to the diameter of the base and height of the cone. From *b* and *d*, as centres, with a radius of 5 feet 8 inches, describe two arcs cutting each other in *e*; then, from *e* as a centre, with the same radius, describe the arc *d f b*; and so on for the other side of the conoid. Perpendicular to the axis *c d*, draw any number of double ordinates *g h*, *i k*; and, from *d'*, No. 5, as a centre, with each of the ordinates as a radius, describe the circles $g^1 h^1$, $i^2 k^2$, the intersection of which with the meridians 1 and 3 will, if projected from the plan to the corresponding line in the elevation, give a point in that line through which the curved meridian line must pass. Thus *i k* is the vertical projection of a circle, of which $i^2 k^2$ is a plan; and the projection of any point *n* in the plan will be found by drawing a line from that point perpendicular to *a b*, cutting *i k* in *o*. Therefore *o* will be one of the points through which the meridian will pass. The same may be said of the great circle *a b*, in which *p* is the projection of point 1.

Through any number of points thus obtained, with the aid of a French curve draw the meridians, as shown by dotted lines in No. 4; and upon *l m* set off the pitch of the screw, which must be divided into eight equal parts, continuing such parts along the line *l m*.

We may now proceed to get in the curvilinear lines of the two blades, commencing at *a* or *b*, precisely in the same manner as for the projection of a common helix (ART. 10).

NOTE.—The only difference in delineating a right or left-hand screw is in the direction of the curve from *a* to *f*. If right-handed, it will pass in front of the axis *c d*; if left-handed, it will pass behind (see No. 6, which is a left-hand screw).

With regard to the plan of No. 4, a simple inspection of No. 5 will show that the convoluted form of the blades is obtained as described for No. 3, or by considering each double ordinate in No. 4 as the elevation of a circle, drawing a plan thereof, and finding the horizontal projection of those points in the ordinates which are intersected by the blades of the screw. (ART. 128, Elem. Treat.)

ART. 26.—A more modern form of propeller than those we have yet described, and the mode of delineating it, will be found on referring to Drawing F, in which No. 1 represents a plan,* No. 2, an end elevation, and No. 3, a side elevation of a propeller which is now to be seen in the Patent Office Museum at South Kensington, and is remarkable from the following printed inscription pasted on one of its blades :—

" SCREW PROPELLER
" of
" H. M. S. RATTLER.

" Weight, 26 cwt. 2 qrs. ; Diameter, 10 ft. 1 in. ; Pitch, 11 feet; Length, 1 ft. 6¾ inches.

" This original screw propeller was tested in Her Majesty's steam sloop ' Rattler,' against the paddle-wheel sloop ' Alecto,' for the purpose of showing the relative towing powers of the screw-propeller and paddle-wheel.

The ' Rattler' being of 888 tons burden, and 200 h.p. The ' Alecto' ,, 800 ,, ,, and 200 h.p.

" This highly interesting and important experiment was made during a perfect calm in the North Sea, on the 3rd

---

* The practice recommended in the Elementary Treatise is to place all elevations of objects in the upper plane, and plans of objects in the lower plane ; the exception to this rule being, when the figures to be introduced make a better or more convenient arrangement by reversing the order, as in this case.

of April, 1845, by lashing the two vessels stern to stern, each exerting their full power in opposite directions, when it was found at the expiration of one hour the 'Rattler' had towed her opponent stern first just two miles and eight-tenths."

ART. 27.—In the previous examples, which have been given for practice in the projection of curved lines, there has been no allusion to the thickness of metal composing the blades, which are made strongest at that point where they join the boss, and gradually tapered off to a feather edge at the outer circumference, and to some extent along the two edges, for the purpose of facilitating their motion through the water; such parts have therefore been represented by single lines.

PROBLEM VII.

Required three views, comprising plan, end, and side elevations of a screw propeller of the following dimensions :—

	ft.	in.
Diameter of screw (left-handed) .	10	1
Pitch of screw	11	0
Breadth of each blade at the widest part (viz., 9 inches from the outer circumference)	4	0
The outer angles of each blade to be rounded with a circle of 7 inches radius.		
Length of screw	1	$6\frac{3}{4}$
Diameter of boss	1	3
Length of boss	1	$10\frac{1}{2}$
Diameter of propeller shaft . . .	0	9

Scale $\frac{1}{2}$ inch to 1 foot.

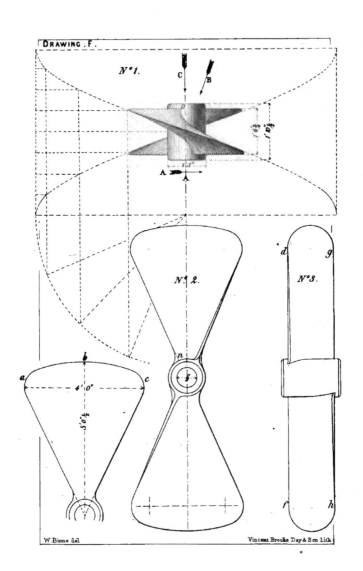

DRAWING. F.

Nº 1.

Nº 2.

Nº 3.

W. Binns del

Vincent Brooks Day & Son Lith.

ART. 28.—With regard to the projection of Nos. 1, 2, 3, Drawing F, which represent three views of the propeller exhibited in the Patent Office Museum, very little need be said, as a recapitulation of the *modus operandi* with helical curves would not only be tedious but unnecessary. We have therefore only to remark that eight points or meridian lines have been used in the semi-circumference (*i.e.* half the pitch), in order to ensure greater accuracy in describing those curves.

Secondly. Having determined the exact size and shape of the blade, as shown at No. 4, the projection of the compound curve forming the periphery, *a b c*, will be found in Nos. 2 and 3, as already described for the projections of a circle. (See PROB. XXIX., Elem. Treat.)

Thirdly. With regard to No. 3. If the blades of an endless screw be cut by two planes which are perpendicular to the axis, it will be manifest that the " trace " of those planes will be represented by lines, *d f, g h,* drawn at right angles to the axis; and the space between those planes, from *d* to *g*, will represent the length of the screw. Also, that the edges of the blades in the end elevation, No. 2, would converge towards the axis, intersecting the boss in point *n*, the plan of which is *o*, the commencement of the curved line on the boss of No. 1. In reality, however, this curve, produced by the intersection of the blade with the boss, is but seldom to be seen, on account of the " ogee " curve formed by the lower portion of the blade with the boss.

ART. 29.—Left-handed screws for propellers. This form or direction of the curve has in all probability been determined upon from the fact that a right-hand or forward motion of the propeller shaft will (with a left-hand screw) produce a forward motion in the vessel, and *vice versâ.* A glance at No. 1, and the arrows A, B, C, will make this quite apparent. If the arrow A represent a right-hand motion of the propeller shaft, the arrow B will represent the direction of resistance which forces the vessel onward in the direction of the arrow c. If we reverse all the arrows the result will be the same, namely a forward motion of the vessel when the propeller moves in the same direction as the hands of a watch, *i.e.* right-handed.

These examples might be multiplied to fill a volume, but enough has been said on the subject to enable the student, with a little application, to find the projection of any one of the very numerous inventions for these instruments of propulsion, which we shall now leave for another part of our subject.

CHAPTER III.

THE COVERINGS OF SOLIDS OF REVOLUTION.

ART. 30.—Certain surfaces of revolution are developable, and others are non-developable. (See Chapter X. Elem. Treat.) Cylinders and cones are the only solids of revolution whose *meridians are right lines*, and they are therefore developable. Solids of revolution having *curved meridians*, such as the sphere, spheroid, conoid, ellipsoid, &c., are non-developable ; that is to say, they are incapable of being entirely or even partially covered with a flexible but non-elastic material, such as paper, zinc, or tin. Gores or strips of such material can, however, be cut into shapes that will approximate very closely to the convex or concave surfaces of solids of revolution having curved meridians ; but it is manifest that the pieces which thus constitute the covering will, in the case of a sphere for example, form a regular spherical polyedron of a certain number of faces, each face being a tangent to the curved surface of the sphere. It is therefore evident that the greater the number of faces, the nearer will the approximation of the polyhedron be to the surface of revolution.

PROBLEM VIII.

Given the radius of a sphere, to find an approximate covering for any part or the whole of its surface.

ART. 31.—With A (No. 1, Drawing G) as a centre, and A B as radius, describe the equatorial circle of the sphere B C D, and draw the diameters B D, C E, at right angles to

each other. Determine the number of gores to be
employed in covering the sphere, say sixteen, and divide
the quadrantal arc B C into a fourth of that number of
equal parts in points 1, 2, 3. Bisect C 3 in e, and make
C f equal to C e. From A, the centre of the sphere, draw
the meridian lines A e, A f, and prolong them to meet a
tangential line, drawn through point C, in G and H. Then
will the isosceles triangle G A H represent the space to be
covered by one of the gores. Prolong A C to F, and make
C F equal to the arc C D. Divide the right line C F and
arc C D each into an equal number of equal parts in
points 5, 6, 7, D, and 5, 6, 7, F. Through each of these
points draw lines parallel to D B, making those lines drawn
from the arc to cut the meridian A e in points i, j, k; the
lines drawn through 5, 6, 7, in C F being of indefinite
length. From the foregoing construction it will be manifest that if the line C F be applied so as to envelop the
sphere, the point F will fall upon the centre A, and the
lines drawn through points 5, 6, 7, on line C F, will coincide
with the corresponding lines drawn from the arc C D.
Now the length of the tangential line is determined by
prolonging the meridians A e, A f, to G and H; it therefore
only remains to make the length of the lines drawn through
points 5, 6, 7, in line C F, each equal to the length of the
corresponding lines contained within the isosceles triangle
G A H, by drawing lines from points i, j, k, parallel to C F,
cutting the lines drawn through points 5, 6, 7, in points
i', j', k', through which the curve F j' G must be drawn,
and the same form of curve repeated on the other side of
line C F. Then will G F H be the form of covering for that
portion of the sphere contained between the lines A G, A H.

It will be understood that the gore G F H will form a
covering for one-sixteenth only of the hemisphere. For
the whole sphere the gores would require to be twice the
length of C F; in which case the sphere, when covered,
would form a regular polyedron of sixteen faces, as shown
on the lower half B E D.

ART. 32.—It is possible that the construction of the foregoing might be attended with inconvenience, on account of the space required for drawing a hemisphere of large dimensions; in such case the following method may be adopted with equal accuracy.

Draw a right line C F (No. 2) equal in length to the quadrantal arc of the hemisphere to be covered. In C F prolonged, take any convenient point A, and draw A B perpendicular to A C. From the centre A, with a radius A C, describe the arc C B. Through C (No. 2) draw G H parallel to A B, and make C G, C H together equal to one face of the polyhedron, as described for No. 1; and join G A. Divide the right line C F and the arc C B (No. 2) each into an equal number of parts in points 1, 2, 3, 4, B, 1, 2, 3, 4, F. Through each point in line C F, draw an indefinite right line parallel to A B; and from 1, 2, 3, 4 in the arc C B draw lines parallel to A B, cutting G A in points i, j, k, l. From these points draw lines parallel to C F, cutting the ordinates in points i', j', k', l', through which the curve F k' G must be drawn; and the operation must be repeated on the right of the line C F. Then will G F H be the development of a portion of the spherical polyhedron, and, when bent as required, will coincide with two of the meridional planes of the sphere,—the angle contained by such planes being determined by dividing 360, the number of degrees in a circle, by the number of gores intended for the covering. Thus for 20 gores we have $\frac{360}{20} = 18°$, and for 36 gores $\frac{360}{36} = 10°$ distant from eacho ther on the equatorial circle, and so on for any number.

This plan of covering a dome is called the *vertical* method. The covering of such a figure, as well as the annulus, and a variety of other figures, may, however, be effected in another way; that is, by dividing the hemisphere by a number of planes drawn perpendicular to the axis, and consequently parallel to the base. This is called the *horizontal* method, and is illustrated by the next problem.

Problem IX.

*Required the forms of covering for a hemispherical dome
when cut by a number of horizontal planes.*

Art. 33.—Let A B C (No. 3, Drawing G) represent
an elevation of the dome to be covered. Bisect A C in D;
and draw D B F perpendicular to A C. Divide the arc B C
into any convenient number of equal parts in points 1, 2,
3, &c., from which draw lines parallel to the base A C. Now
conceive the space between each horizontal section to form
the frustum of a cone, and proceed to find the development
thereof as directed by Art. 162, Elem. Treat.; that is,
through points 4 and 5 draw a right line cutting the axial
line in F; and with F as a centre, and F 4, F 5 as radii,
describe two arcs of circles, which will give the form of
covering for that portion of the spherical surface contained
by the two parallel lines drawn from points 4 and 5; and
so on with the other portions of the figure.

Art. 34.—No. 4, Drawing G, shows the same method
applied to the covering for an ellipsoidal dome, which will
be readily understood from the construction lines and the
above description of No. 3.

Problem X.

Required the form of covering for an annular vault.

Art. 35.—Let E A, No. 5, Drawing G, be the outer
diameter; D B the inner diameter; C the centre; and B A
the thickness of the annulus. Bisect B A in g; and from
g, as a centre, describe the semicircle B h A, which will
represent a section of the annulus. From C, as centre,

and with c a, c b as radii, describe two semicircles
a i e, b h d, to represent a semi-plan of the annulus.
Divide the circumference of the semicircle b *h* a into
any convenient number of equal parts, 1, 2, 3, &c.; and
through c draw i c f perpendicular to e a. Through
any two consecutive points in the arc b *h* a, as 3, 2, draw
a right line cutting c f in *k*; and from *k*, as a centre, with
k 3, *k* 2 as radii, describe two arcs of circles, which will
give the contour of the covering for a portion of the
annulus contained within the semicircles 3′ 2′; and so on
with every portion of the annulus, as shown by the lines
of construction.

When it is remembered that the line i f represents the
vertical axis of the annulus, of which b *h* a is a vertical
section, the mode of construction will be clearly understood.

Art. 36.—Before leaving the subject of the sphere,
it may be desirable to bring to the notice of the student a
mode of setting out the plates of a cylindrical steam boiler
with hemispherical ends. The writer's attention having
been called to this problem, on account of a want of
clearness and some inaccuracy in the drawings given in
other works on this subject, he has been induced to
attempt a more lucid description, and to make some
alteration in the mode of working out the problem.
Moreover the gores, from three to eight in number
(depending upon the diameter of the boiler), are much
larger than those employed in the foregoing illustrations
of the sphere, and therefore require some modification in
the mode of finding their projection, which the student
may take as an exercise before referring to the text and
drawings of the following problem.

PROBLEM XI.

Required the form and size of a plate suitable for one of the gores of a boiler with hemispherical ends. The number of gores being six; the diameter of boiler, 4 feet 6 inches; and length of plates, 3 feet. Scale, $\frac{4}{8}$ of an inch to 1 foot.

ART. 37.—Draw the centre line of construction A C B, No. 6, Drawing G. From any point C, with a radius of 2 feet 3 inches ($\frac{4}{8}$ scale), draw a circle to represent the end of the boiler; and from any point B, with the same radius, draw a semicircle to represent a sectional plan of the same. Divide the circle *a b c* into six equal parts; and from the centre C, draw C *b*, C *c*. Upon the arc of the semicircle set off D E equal to the length of the plate; then divide D E into any number of equal parts 1, 2, &c., and draw the ordinates 1 *e*, 2 *e*, &c. From C as a centre, and with the radius *e* 1, *e* 2, &c., describe the arcs *f* 1, *f* 2, &c., as indicated by dotted lines drawn from 1 and 2 parallel to A B. Upon any right line, as C F, set off *g h*, equal to the length of the arc D E, and divide *g h* into the same number of equal parts as D E, in points 1′, 2′, &c., through which draw double ordinates perpendicular to C F, making them equal in length to the corresponding arcs *f* 1, *f* 2, &c. These lengths may be obtained by calculation; but for all practical purposes it will be sufficient to divide, with a pair of compasses, the arc *f* 1 into three or four equal parts, and set such parts off on the right line 1′ *f*′; and proceed in like manner with the other lines. Through the points *k*′, *f*′, *b*′, thus found, draw the curve *k*′ *b*′, also *i*′ *c*′, which will give the form of plate required for one of the gores; allowance being made for the rivets and over-lapping of the joints, which will be understood. In the process of manufacture these plates are heated, and then hammered upon a concave surface to give them the necessary sphericity.

CHAPTER IV.

Toothed Wheels and their Pitch.

ART. 38.—Toothed wheels are employed for transmitting motion, regulating velocity, and converting one species of motion into another; consequently, they are variously formed and designated. Those that come more immediately under the general term of "gearing," as applied to mill-work, are known as spur wheels, pinions, mortise wheels, bevel wheels, mitre wheels, crown wheels, and worm wheels. There are also others, termed elliptical wheels, spiral wheels, and skew gear, which, with the mangle wheel and ratchet wheel, will be explained in a future Chapter.

ART. 39.—Spur wheels, sometimes called "spur gear," are those that transmit motion to lines of shafts which are parallel to each other. They are said to be *in gear* when their teeth are engaged, and *out of gear* when their teeth are apart. Spur wheels are often represented by circles (as in Fig. 3), whose diameters are to one another as their intended velocities.

Fig. 3.

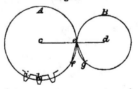

Thus A and B are called the *pitch circles*, but more commonly the *pitch lines* of the wheels, and, when in gear, must be drawn to touch each other at their circumferences. The right line *c d*, drawn from centre to centre, is called the *line of centres*; and the radii of the two circles *d e, c e*, the *proportional radii*. The pitch circles therefore form the basis of all calculations as regards the

D

diameter, number of teeth, and *pitch* of wheels.   On this subject it is deemed necessary to offer some remarks, first observing that a " pinion" is a small wheel, spur or otherwise, with, say 12 or 14 teeth; but this term, however, is frequently applied to the smallest of two or more geared wheels, irrespective of size or number of teeth.

ART. 40.—The *pitch* of a wheel is the distance from centre to centre, *i* to *k*, Fig. 3, of two contiguous teeth, and therefore equal to the thickness of a tooth and a space or interval between two teeth; and, although mathematicians have clearly demonstrated that such distance must be measured on the circumference or *arc* of the pitch circle, we still meet with cases in which this theory is set aside by the use of tables which presuppose that a wheel is a polygon of as many sides as there are teeth, and that each side of the polygon, or, in other words, *the chord of the arc, is the true pitch.* Now this would imply that, if the chords *e f* and *e g*, Fig. 3, are equal, the arcs of those chords will be equal, the diameters of the circles being unequal!—which is impossible.   For the benefit of those who still practise and believe in the *chord* principle, we will endeavour to show that the tables referred to are not in accordance with the principles of rolling contact.

ART. 41.—In the first place, the circumference of a circle is to the diameter as 3·14159 to 1; *i. e.* the diameter being 1 foot or 1 inch, the circumference will be 3·14159 feet or inches.   The symbol for this number is the Greek letter π; and in mechanical calculations it is always taken to represent the number 3·1416.

ART. 42.—Taking for granted that the rolling motion

---

* *Vide* Templeton's " Millwright and Engineer's Pocket Companion," p. 118, also " The Mechanic's Calculator," by W. Grier, p. 183, where it is said, " The true pitch is a straight line, but these rules give it an arc of the circle which passes through the centre of the teeth, whereas it should be the *chord* of the arc."

of the pitch lines of a pair of wheels ought to be precisely the same as if they were a pair of cylinders, void of teeth— except the very minute and innumerable projections which cause them to revolve by the friction of rolling contact— any two points on their peripheries, each touching the line of centres, would, in the case of a pair of wheels whose radii or circumferences are as 1, always meet on the line of centres. If the radii or circumferences were as 3 to 1, the two points would meet on that line at every revolution of the large wheel, and every third revolution of the smaller wheel. Although it has been stated that the action of the smoothest working wheels is still a stepping motion, that practically answers the end of purely rolling contact, there is no reason why we should have a jumping motion, that practically ends in a series of jolts; but this is what the writer has met with; and he is therefore desirous of showing, in the most simple manner, how far the conditions of rolling contact agree with the tables referred to, of which it is said, " It will be easy to determine the diameter of any wheel, having the pitch and number of teeth in that wheel given,"—the rule being as follows:—

" Multiply the radius in the table by the pitch given, and the product will be the radius of the wheel."

ART. 43.—Let us take for example a wheel with 24 teeth $3\frac{1}{2}$ inches pitch. Opposite the number 24, in the tables referred to, will be found 3·830, a factor, which multiplied by 3·5 $= 13·405$ inches, the radius of the wheel ; and $13·405 \times 2 \times \pi = 84·226$ inches, the circumference. But from what has been said (ART. 40) the circumference of a wheel having 24 teeth $3\frac{1}{2}$ inches pitch must be 24 times $3\frac{1}{2}$ inches, which is exactly 84 inches ; consequently, we have, in the tables before us, a difference of 0·226, or *very nearly a quarter of an inch,* in the circumference of a wheel of little more than 26 inches diameter.

Suppose the above wheel were required to work with a wheel of 150 teeth. Calculating from the same table we find the circumference to be $23\cdot875 \times 3\cdot5 \times 2 \times 3\cdot1416$ $= 525\cdot04$ inches, being only the 25th part of an inch larger in circumference than the correct measurement, which in practice is inappreciable. This close approximation is owing to the arc of the circle between the centres of two contiguous teeth approaching so near to a right line. It may be said that there is, in practice, little or no objection to the rules and tables of Templeton, Wallace, Brunton, Grier, and others, when calculating wheels of large diameter. It must be remembered, however, that large wheels are often required to work with small ones, and whether large or small, they ought to be correct. But wheels constructed from these tables are not so. Take two discs, accurately calculated from the above-mentioned tables of $3\frac{1}{4}$ inches pitch, one with 24 equal divisions, and the other with 150, to represent respectively the numbers of teeth before named, and place them together each with a point or division on the line of centres. If motion be now given them by the friction of rolling contact, it will be found that the divisions will go on separating, so that with one revolution of the small wheel the points representing *the centres of the teeth will be* $0\cdot226$ *of an inch apart,* and for one revolution of the large wheel we shall have $\dfrac{150}{24} = 6\cdot25 \times \cdot226 = 1\ 4$ inch as the amount of separation of points which in properly constructed wheels will meet for any number of revolutions. The effect of pitching wheels upon the *chord* principle instead of the *arc* is an unnecessary amount of friction, abrasion, and jolting.

ART. 44.—To show some of the evils resulting from badly constructed wheels, especially when small and of coarse pitch, it may be stated that a few years since the writer was consulted by the plaintiff in an action to recover damages for loss of time and expense of repairs to a machine for planing wood, in which occasional breakages, with a jolting noise, and wave-like appearance on the surface of the planed board were complained of. Having arrived at the conclusion that the defect was in the gearing, the writer ordered two wooden discs to be made, of the same diameter as the pitch circles of the defective wheel and pinion, and, on the faces of the discs, which were covered with white paper, he carefully set off with radial lines the pitch or divisions of the teeth. The illustration of this model by rolling contact was sufficient to convince the jury that wheels so constructed could not work without abrasion and other injurious effects; and the result was a verdict for the plaintiff, with damages and all costs. It will therefore be seen that a knowledge of the principles of construction and action of a pair of wheels can be very dearly bought; and it is for this and other reasons that attention is particularly directed to the following formulæ:—

ART. 45.—*Formulæ for calculating the pitch, diameter, and number of teeth of wheels, wherein p = pitch, d = diameter, and n = number of teeth.*

$$p = \frac{d\,\pi}{n} \qquad (1)$$

$$d = \frac{n\,p}{\pi} \qquad (2)$$

$$n = \frac{d\,\pi}{p} \qquad (3)$$

Or in words, the rules for finding the pitch, diameter, and number of teeth are as follow:—

1st. The diameter and number of teeth being given, to find the pitch.

Multiply the diameter by 3·1416, and divide the product by the number of teeth, the quotient will be the pitch (1).

2nd. The number of teeth and pitch being given, to find the diameter.

Multiply the number of teeth by the pitch, and divide the product by 3·1416, the quotient will be the diameter (2).

3rd. The diameter and pitch being given, to find the number of teeth.

Multiply the diameter by 3·1416, and divide the product by the pitch, the quotient will be the number of teeth (3).

Example 1.—What will be the pitch of a wheel whose diameter is 26¾ inches and number of teeth 24?

$$(1.) \qquad \frac{26\cdot75 \times 3\cdot1416}{24} = 3\cdot5 \text{ inches pitch.}$$

Example 2.—What will be the diameter of a wheel with 35 teeth, the pitch being 2 inches?

$$(2.) \qquad \frac{35 \times 2}{3\cdot1416} = 22\cdot281 \text{ inches diameter.}$$

Example 3.—What will be the number of teeth in a wheel whose diameter is 42 inches and pitch 2½ inches?

$$(3.) \qquad \frac{42 \times 3\cdot1416}{2\cdot5} = 52\cdot779 \text{ teeth.}$$

In this last example we have got a fraction (·779) of a tooth, which is not admissible, as the teeth of a wheel *must be a whole number.* It therefore becomes necessary to alter the diameter of the pitch circle, and, by Example 2, we get

$$\frac{53 \times 2\cdot5}{3\cdot1416} = 42\cdot176 \text{ inches}$$

for the diameter of a wheel to contain 53 teeth 2½ inches pitch.

ART. 46.—The foregoing rules have been somewhat abridged, by calculating beforehand the values of $\frac{p}{\pi}$ and $\frac{\pi}{p}$ corresponding to the pitches from ¼ inch to 6 inches, as given in the following table, which, it is said, will be found very convenient when the diameter d is to be determined, the pitch p and number of teeth n being given; and conversely, when the diameter and pitch are given, to find the number of teeth.

Table for calculating the diameter and number of teeth when the pitch of wheel is given :—

Pitch in inches and parts of an inch.	$D = \frac{P}{\pi} \times N$ RULE.—To find the diameter in inches, multiply the number of teeth by the tabular number answering to the given pitch.	$N = \frac{\pi}{P} \times D$ RULE.—To find the number of teeth, multiply the given diameter in inches by the tabular number answering to the given pitch.
Values of P	Values of $\frac{P}{\pi}$	Values of $\frac{\pi}{P}$
6	1·9095	·5236
5	1·5915	·6283
4½	1·4270	·6981
4	1·2732	·7854
3½	1·1141	·8976
3	·9547	1·0472
2¾	·8754	1·1424
2½	·7958	1·2566
2¼	·7135	1·3963
2	·6366	1·5708
1⅞	·5937	1·6755
1¾	·5570	1·7952
1⅝	·5141	1·9264
1½	·4774	2·0944
1⅜	·4377	2·2848
1¼	·3979	2·5132
1⅛	·3568	2·7926
1	·3183	3·1416
⅞	·2785	3·5904
¾	·2387	4·1888
⅝	·1989	5·0266
½	·1592	6·2832
⅜	·1194	8·3776
¼	·0796	12·5664

ART. 47.—The use of this table will be understood from the following examples :—

1. Given a wheel of 53 teeth 2½ inches pitch, to find the diameter of the pitch circle. Here the tabular number in the second column answering to the given pitch is ·7958, which multiplied by 53 gives 42·177, the diameter required. This is correct within an exceedingly small fraction, 42·176 being the right diameter.

2. What will be the number of teeth in a wheel of 45 inches diameter and 2¾ inches pitch? The factor in the third column corresponding to the given pitch is 1·1424, which multiplied by 45 gives 51·408 for the number of teeth.

Here again we have a fraction (·408) of a tooth, which must be cancelled, and 51 or 52 teeth assigned; in either case the diameter of the pitch circle must be altered. Thus, by Example 1, we have in the second column ·8754 × 51 = 44·645 for the diameter of a wheel of 51 teeth 2¾ inches pitch.

ART. 48.—In designing machinery and checking calculations like the above, the following comprehensive table will be found of great service, inasmuch as it gives, by inspection, the diameters, in inches, of wheels, from 10 to 340 teeth, and from 1¼ to 3½ inches pitch. The table, with some corrections, has been taken from Grier's valuable " Mechanic's Pocket Dictionary."

OF TOOTHED WHEELS.

Table of the *Diameters, in inches, of Wheels, from* 10 to 340 *teeth, a* 1¼ *to* 3½ *inches pitch.*

Number of Teeth	Pitch. 1¼ Diam.	Pitch. 1½ Diam.	Pitch. 1¾ Diam.	Pitch. 2 Diam.	Pitch. 2¼ Diam.	Pitch. 2½ Diam.	Pitch. 2¾ Diam.	Pitch. 3 Diam.	Pitch. 3½ Diam.
10	3·978	4·774	5·570	6·366	7·161	7·957	8·753	9·549	10·345
11	4·376	5·252	6·127	7·002	7·878	8·753	9·628	10·504	11·379
12	4·774	5·729	6·684	7·639	8·594	9·549	10·504	11·459	12·414
13	5·172	6·267	7·241	8·276	9·310	10·345	11·379	12·414	13·448
14	5·570	6·684	7·798	8·912	10·026	11·140	12·254	13·368	14·482
15	5·968	7·161	8·355	9·549	10·742	11·936	13·130	14·324	15·517
16	6·366	7·639	8·912	10·185	11·459	12·732	14·005	15·278	16·552
17	6·764	8·116	9·469	10·822	12·175	13·528	14·880	16·233	17·586
18	7·161	8·594	10·026	11·459	12·891	14·324	15·756	17·188	18·621
19	7·559	9·071	10·583	12·095	13·607	15·119	16·631	18·143	19·655
20	7·957	9·549	11·140	12·732	14·324	15·915	17·507	19·098	20·690
21	8·355	10·026	11·697	13·368	15·040	16·711	18·382	20·053	21·724
22	8·753	10·504	12·254	14·005	15·756	17·507	19·257	21·008	22·759
23	9·151	10·981	12·811	14·641	16·472	18·303	20·132	21·963	23·793
24	9·549	11·459	13·368	15·278	17·188	19·098	21·008	22·918	24·828
25	9·947	11·936	13·926	15·915	17·905	19·894	21·883	23·873	25·862
26	10·345	12·414	14·483	16·552	18·621	20·690	22·759	24·828	26·897
27	10·742	12·891	15·040	17·188	19·337	21·485	23·634	25·783	27·931
28	11·140	13·368	15·596	17·824	20·053	22·281	24·509	26·738	28·966
29	11·518	13·845	16·153	18·460	20·770	23·077	25·384	27·693	30·000
30	11·936	14·324	16·711	19·098	21·485	23·873	26·260	28·647	31·035
31	12·334	14·801	17·268	19·734	22·202	24·668	27·135	29·602	32·069
32	12·732	15·278	17·824	20·370	22·918	25·464	28·010	30·557	33·104
33	13·130	15·755	18·382	21·008	23·635	26·260	28·885	31·512	34·139
34	13·528	16·233	18·939	21·644	24·352	27·056	29·760	32·468	35·173
35	13·926	16·711	19·496	22·281	25·069	27·852	30·635	33·423	36·208
36	14·324	17·188	20·053	22·918	25·783	28·647	31·512	34·377	37·242
37	14·722	17·666	20·610	23·554	26·499	29·443	32·387	35·332	38·276
38	15·119	18·143	21·167	24·191	27·215	30·239	33·263	36·287	39·311
39	15·517	18·621	21·724	24·828	27·931	31·035	34·138	37·242	40·345
40	15·915	19·098	22·281	25·464	28·647	31·830	35·014	38·197	41·380
41	16·313	19·575	22·838	26·101	29·363	32·626	35·889	39·151	42·414
42	16·711	20·053	23·395	26·737	30·080	33·422	36·764	40·106	43·449
43	17·109	20·530	23·952	27·374	30·796	34·218	37·640	41·061	44·483
44	17·507	21·008	24·509	28·011	31·512	35·013	38·515	42·016	45·518
45	17·905	21·485	25·066	28·647	32·228	35·809	39·390	42·971	46·552
46	18·303	21·963	25·623	29·284	32·944	36·605	40·266	43·926	47·587
47	18·700	22·440	26·180	29·920	33·661	37·401	41·141	44·881	48·621
48	19·098	22·918	26·737	30·557	34·377	38·197	42·016	45·836	49·656
49	19·496	23·395	27·294	31·194	35·093	38·992	42·892	46·791	50·690
50	19·894	23·873	27·852	31·830	35·809	39·788	43·767	47·746	51·725
51	20·292	24·350	28·409	32·467	36·525	40·584	44·642	48·701	52·759
52	20·690	24·828	28·966	33·104	37·242	41·380	45·518	49·656	53·794
53	21·088	25·305	29·523	33·740	37·958	42·175	46·393	50·611	54·828
54	21·486	25·782	30·080	34·377	38·674	42·971	47·268	51·565	55·863
55	21·884	26·260	30·637	35·013	39·390	43·767	48·144	52·520	56·897
56	22·281	26·737	31·194	35·650	40·106	44·563	49·019	53·475	57·932
57	22·679	27·215	31·751	36·287	40·823	45·358	49·894	54·430	58·966
58	23·077	27·692	32·308	36·923	41·539	46·154	50·770	55·385	60·001
59	23·475	28·170	32·865	37·560	42·255	46·950	51·645	56·340	61·035
60	23·873	28·647	33·422	38·197	42·971	47·746	52·520	57·295	62·070
61	24·271	29·125	33·979	38·833	43·687	48·542	53·395	58·250	63·104
62	24·668	29·602	34·536	39·470	44·404	49·337	54·271	59·205	64·139
63	25·066	30·080	35·093	40·106	45·120	50·133	55·146	60·160	65·173
64	25·464	30·557	35·650	40·743	45·836	50·929	56·021	61·115	66·208
65	25·862	31·035	36·207	41·380	46·552	51·725	56·897	62·070	67·242
66	26·260	31·512	36·764	42·016	47·268	52·520	57·772	63·025	68·277
67	26·658	31·990	37·321	42·653	47·985	53·316	58·648	63·980	69·311
68	27·056	32·467	37·878	43·289	48·701	54·112	59·523	64·935	70·346
69	27·454	32·944	38·435	43·926	49·417	54·908	60·398	65·889	71·380
70	27·851	33·422	38·992	44·563	50·133	55·704	61·274	66·844	72·415
71	28·249	33·899	39·549	45·199	50·849	56·499	62·149	67·799	73·449
72	28·647	34·377	40·106	45·836	51·566	57·295	63·025	68·754	74·484

Table of the Diameters of Wheels, continued.

Number of Teeth	Pitch 1¼ Diam.	Pitch 1½ Diam.	Pitch 1¾ Diam.	Pitch 2 Diam.	Pitch 2¼ Diam.	Pitch 2½ Diam.	Pitch 2¾ Diam.	Pitch 3 Diam.	Pitch 3¼ Diam.	Pitch 3½ Diam.
73	29·045	34·854	40·663	46·473	52·282	58·091	63·900	69·709	75·518	81·327
74	29·443	35·332	41·220	47·109	52·998	58·837	64·775	70·664	76·553	82·442
75	29·841	35·809	41·778	47·746	53·714	59·682	65·651	71·619	77·587	83·556
76	30·239	36·287	42·335	48·382	54·430	60·478	66·526	72·574	78·622	84·670
77	30·637	36·764	42·892	49·019	55·146	61·274	67·401	73·529	79·656	85·784
78	31·034	37·242	43·449	49·656	55·863	62·070	68·277	74·484	80·691	86·898
79	31·432	37·719	44·006	50·292	56·579	62·866	69·152	75·439	81·725	88·012
80	31·830	38·197	44·563	50·929	57·295	63·661	70·028	76·394	82·760	89·126
81	32·228	38·674	45·120	51·565	58·011	64·457	70·903	77·349	83·794	90·240
82	32·626	39·151	45·677	52·202	58·727	65·253	71·778	78·304	84·829	91·354
83	33·024	39·629	46·234	52·839	59·444	66·049	72·654	79·258	85·863	92·468
84	33·422	40·106	46·791	53·475	60·160	66·844	73·529	80·213	86·898	93·582
85	33·820	40·584	47·348	54·112	60·876	67·640	74·404	81·168	87·932	94·696
86	34·218	41·061	47·905	54·748	61·592	68·436	75·280	82·123	88·967	95·810
87	34·615	41·539	48·462	55·385	62·308	69·232	76·155	83·078	90·001	96·925
88	35·013	42·016	49·019	56·022	63·025	70·027	77·030	84·033	91·036	98·039
89	35·411	42·494	49·576	56·658	63·741	70·823	77·906	84·988	92·070	99·153
90	35·809	42·971	50·133	57·295	64·457	71·619	78·781	85·943	93·105	100·267
91	36·207	43·449	50·690	57·932	65·173	72·415	79·656	86·898	94·139	101·381
92	36·605	43·926	51·247	58·568	65·889	73·211	80·532	87·853	95·174	102·495
93	37·003	44·404	51·804	59·205	66·606	74·006	81·407	88·808	96·208	103·609
94	37·401	44·881	52·361	59·841	67·322	74·802	82·282	89·763	97·243	104·723
95	37·798	45·358	52·918	60·478	68·038	75·598	83·158	90·717	98·277	105·837
96	38·196	45·836	53·475	61·115	68·754	76·394	84·033	91·672	99·312	106·951
97	38·594	46·313	54·032	61·751	69·470	77·189	84·908	92·627	100·346	108·065
98	38·992	46·791	54·589	62·388	70·186	77·985	85·784	93·582	101·381	109·179
99	39·390	47·268	55·146	63·024	70·903	78·781	86·659	94·537	102·415	110·294
100	39·788	47·746	55·704	63·661	71·619	79·577	87·585	95·492	103·450	111·408
101	40·186	48·223	56·261	64·298	72·335	80·373	88·410	96·447	104·484	112·522
102	40·584	48·701	56·818	64·935	73·051	81·168	89·285	97·402	105·519	113·636
103	40·982	49·178	57·375	65·571	73·768	81·964	90·161	98·357	106·553	114·750
104	41·380	49·656	57·932	66·208	74·484	82·760	91·036	99·312	107·588	115·864
105	41·778	50·133	58·489	66·844	75·200	83·556	91·911	100·267	108·622	116·978
106	42·175	50·611	59·046	67·481	75·916	84·351	92·787	101·222	109·657	118·092
107	42·573	51·088	59·603	68·118	76·632	85·147	93·662	102·177	110·691	119·206
108	42·971	51·566	60·160	68·754	77·349	85·943	94·537	103·133	111·726	120·320
109	43·369	52·043	60·717	69·391	78·065	86·739	95·413	104·087	112·760	121·434
110	43·767	52·520	61·274	70·027	78·781	87·534	96·288	105·042	113·795	122·548
111	44·165	52·998	61·831	70·664	79·497	88·330	97·163	105·996	114·829	123·663
112	44·563	53·475	62·388	71·301	80·213	89·126	98·039	106·951	115·864	124·777
113	44·960	53·953	62·945	71·937	80·930	89·922	98·914	107·906	116·898	125·891
114	45·358	54·430	63·502	72·574	81·646	90·718	99·789	108·861	117·933	127·005
115	45·756	54·908	64·059	73·210	82·362	91·513	100·665	109·816	118·967	128·119
116	46·154	55·385	64·616	73·847	83·078	92·309	101·540	110·771	120·002	129·233
117	46·551	55·863	65·173	74·484	83·794	93·105	102·415	111·726	121·036	130·347
118	46·950	56·340	65·730	75·120	84·510	93·901	103·291	112·681	122·071	131·461
119	47·348	56·818	66·287	75·757	85·227	94·696	104·166	113·636	123·105	132·575
120	47·746	57·295	66·844	76·394	85·943	95·492	105·042	114·591	124·140	133·689
121	48·144	57·773	67·401	77·030	86·659	96·288	105·917	115·546	125·175	134·803
122	48·542	58·250	67·958	77·667	87·375	97·084	106·792	116·501	126·209	135·918
123	48·939	58·728	68·516	78·303	88·091	97·880	107·668	117·456	127·244	137·032
124	49·337	59·205	69·073	78·940	88·808	98·675	108·543	118·410	128·278	138·146
125	49·735	59·682	69·630	79·577	89·524	99·471	109·418	119·365	129·313	139·260
126	50·133	60·160	70·187	80·213	90·240	100·267	110·294	120·320	130·347	140·374
127	50·531	60·637	70·744	80·850	90·956	101·063	111·169	121·275	131·382	141·488
128	50·929	61·115	71·301	81·486	91·672	101·858	112·044	122·230	132·416	142·602
129	51·327	61·592	71·858	82·123	92·389	102·654	112·920	123·185	133·451	143·716
130	51·725	62·070	72·415	82·760	93·105	103·450	113·795	124·140	134·485	144·830
131	52·122	62·547	72·972	83·396	93·821	104·246	114·670	125·095	135·520	145·944
132	52·520	63·025	73·529	84·033	94·537	105·042	115·546	126·050	136·554	147·058
133	52·918	63·502	74·086	84·670	95·254	105·837	116·421	127·005	137·589	148·172
134	53·316	63·980	74·643	85·306	95·971	106·633	117·296	127·960	138·623	149·287
135	53·714	64·457	75·200	85·943	96·687	107·429	118·172	128·915	139·658	150·401
136	54·112	64·935	75·757	86·579	97·403	108·225	119·047	129·870	140·692	151·515
137	54·510	65·412	76·314	87·216	98·119	109·020	119·922	130·824	141·727	152·629
138	54·908	65·890	76·871	87·853	98·835	109·816	120·798	131·779	142·761	153·743
139	55·305	66·367	77·428	88·489	99·551	110·612	121·673	132·734	143·796	154·857

Table of the Diameters of Wheels, continued.

Number of Teeth	Pitch. 1¼ Diam.	Pitch. 1½ Diam.	Pitch. 1¾ Diam.	Pitch. 2 Diam.	Pitch. 2¼ Diam.	Pitch. 2½ Diam.	Pitch. 2¾ Diam.	Pitch. 3 Diam.	Pitch. 3¼ Diam.	Pitch. 3½ Diam.
140	55·703	66·844	77·985	89·126	100·267	111·408	122·548	133·689	144·830	155·971
141	56·101	67·322	78·542	89·762	100·983	112·203	123·424	134·644	145·865	157·085
142	56·499	67·799	79·099	90·399	101·699	112·999	124·299	135·599	146·899	158·199
143	56·897	68·277	79·656	91·036	102·415	113·796	125·174	136·554	147·934	159·313
144	57·295	68·754	80·213	91·673	103·132	114·591	126·050	137·509	148·968	160·427
145	57·693	69·232	80·770	92·309	103·848	115·387	126·925	138·464	150·003	161·541
146	58·091	69·709	81·327	92·946	104·564	116·182	127·801	139·419	151·037	162·655
147	58·489	70·187	81·884	93·582	105·280	116·978	128·676	140·374	152·072	163·770
148	58·887	70·664	82·442	94·219	105·996	117·774	129·551	141·329	153·106	164·884
149	59·285	71·142	82·999	94·855	106·713	118·570	130·427	142·284	154·141	165·998
150	59·682	71·619	83·556	95·492	107·429	119·365	131·302	143·239	155·175	167·112
151	60·080	72·097	84·113	96·129	108·145	120·161	132·177	144·193	156·210	168·226
152	60·478	72·574	84·670	96·765	108·861	120·957	133·053	145·148	157·244	169·340
153	60·876	73·051	85·227	97·402	109·577	121·753	133·928	146·103	158·279	170·454
154	61·274	73·529	85·784	98·039	110·294	122·548	134·803	147·058	159·313	171·568
155	61·672	74·006	86·341	98·675	111·010	123·344	135·679	148·013	160·348	172·682
156	62·070	74·484	86·898	99·312	111·726	124·140	136·554	148·968	161·382	173·796
157	62·468	74·961	87·455	99·948	112·442	124·936	137·429	149·923	162·417	174·910
158	62·865	75·439	88·012	100·585	113·158	125·732	138·305	150·878	163·451	176·024
159	63·263	75·916	88·569	101·222	113·875	126·527	139·180	151·833	164·486	177·139
160	63·661	76·394	89·126	101·858	114·591	127·323	140·056	152·788	165·520	178·253
161	64·059	76·871	89·683	102·495	115·307	128·119	140·931	153·743	166·559	179·367
162	64·457	77·349	90·240	103·132	116·023	128·915	141·806	154·698	167·585	180·481
163	64·855	77·826	90·797	103·768	116·739	129·710	142·682	155·653	168·624	181·595
164	65·253	78·303	91·354	104·405	117·455	130·506	143·557	156·607	169·658	182·709
165	65·651	78·781	91·911	105·041	118·171	131·302	144·432	157·562	170·693	183·823
166	66·049	79·258	92·468	105·678	118·888	132·098	145·308	158·517	171·727	184·937
167	66·446	79·736	93·025	106·315	119·604	132·893	146·183	159·472	172·762	186·051
168	66·844	80·213	93·582	106·951	120·320	133·689	147·058	160·427	173·796	187·165
169	67·242	80·601	94·139	107·588	121·036	134·485	147·934	161·382	174·831	188·279
170	67·640	81·168	94·696	108·225	121·753	135·281	148·809	162·337	175·865	189·393
171	68·038	81·646	95·253	108·862	122·469	136·077	149·684	163·292	176·900	190·508
172	68·436	82·123	95·811	109·499	123·185	136·872	150·560	164·247	177·934	191·622
173	68·834	82·601	96·368	110·135	123·901	137·668	151·435	165·202	178·969	192·736
174	69·232	83·078	96·925	110·772	124·617	138·464	152·310	166·157	180·003	193·850
175	69·629	83·556	97·482	111·408	125·334	139·260	153·186	167·112	181·038	194·964
176	70·027	84·033	98·039	112·045	126·050	140·055	154·061	168·067	182·072	196·078
177	70·425	84·510	98·596	112·682	126·766	140·851	154·936	169·022	183·107	197·192
178	70·823	84·988	99·153	113·3,8	127·482	141·647	155·812	169·977	184·141	198·306
179	71·221	85·465	99·710	113·955	128·198	142·443	156·687	170·931	185·176	199·420
180	71·619	85·943	100·267	114·591	128·915	143·239	157·563	171·886	186·210	200·534
181	72·017	86·420	100·824	115·227	129·631	144·034	158·438	172·841	187·245	201·648
182	72·415	86·898	101·381	115·864	130·347	144·830	159·313	173·796	188·279	202·762
183	72·813	87·375	101·938	116·501	131·063	145·626	160·189	174·751	189·314	203·876
184	73·211	87·853	102·495	117·137	131·779	146·422	161·064	175·706	190·348	204·991
185	73·608	88·330	103·052	117·774	132·496	147·217	161·939	176·661	191·383	206·105
186	74·006	88·808	103·609	118·410	133·212	148·013	162·815	177·616	192·417	207·219
187	74·404	89·285	104·166	119·047	133·928	148·809	163·690	178·571	193·452	208·333
188	74·802	89·763	104·723	119·684	134·644	149·605	164·565	179·526	194·486	209·447
189	75·200	90·240	105·280	120·320	135·360	150·401	165·441	180·481	195·521	210·561
190	75·598	90·718	105·837	120·957	136·077	151·196	166·316	181·436	196·555	211·675
191	75·996	91·195	106·394	121·593	136·743	151·992	167·191	182·391	197·590	212·789
192	76·394	91·673	106·951	122·230	137·509	152·788	168·067	183·346	198·624	213·903
193	76·732	92·150	107·508	122·867	138·225	153·584	168·942	184·300	199·659	215·017
194	77·189	92·627	108·065	123·503	138·941	154·379	169·817	185·255	200·693	216·131
195	77·587	93·105	108·622	124·140	139·658	155·175	170·693	186·210	201·728	217·245
196	77·985	93·582	109·180	124·777	140·374	155·971	171·568	187·165	202·762	218·360
197	78·383	94·060	109·737	125·413	141·090	156·767	172·444	188·120	203·797	219·474
198	78·781	94·537	110·294	126·050	141·806	157·563	173·319	189·075	204·831	220·588
199	79·179	95·015	110·851	126·686	142·522	158·358	174·194	190·030	205·886	221·702
200	79·577	95·492	111·408	127·323	143·239	159·154	175·070	190·985	206·900	222·816
201	79·975	95·970	111·965	127·960	143·955	159·950	175·945	191·949	207·935	223·930
202	80·372	96·447	112·522	128·596	144·671	160·746	176·820	192·895	208·969	225·044
203	80·770	96·925	113·079	129·233	145·387	161·541	177·696	193·850	210·004	226·158
204	81·168	97·402	113·636	129·870	146·103	162·337	178·571	194·805	211·038	227·272
205	81·566	97·880	114·193	130·506	146·820	163·133	179·446	195·760	212·073	228·386
206	81·964	98·357	114·750	131·143	147·536	163·929	180·322	196·714	213·107	229·500

Table of the Diameters of Wheels, continued.

Number of Teeth	Pitch. 1¼	Pitch. 1½	Pitch. 1¾	Pitch. 2	Pitch. 2¼	Pitch. 2½	Pitch. 2¾	Pitch. 3	Pitch. 3¼	Pitch. 3½
	Diam.	Diam.	Diam.	Diam.	Diam.	Diam.	Diam.	Diam.	Diam.	Diam.
207	82·362	98·834	115·307	131·779	148·252	164·724	181·197	197·669	214·142	230·614
208	82·760	99·312	115·864	132·416	148·968	165·520	182·072	198·624	215·176	231·729
209	83·158	99·789	116·421	133·053	149·684	166·316	182·948	199·579	216·211	232·843
210	83·556	100·267	116·978	133·686	150·400	167·112	183·823	200·534	217·245	233·957
211	83·953	100·744	117·535	134·329	151·117	167·908	184·698	201·489	218·280	235·071
212	84·351	101·222	118·092	134·963	151·833	168·703	185·574	202·444	219·314	236·185
213	84·749	101·699	118·649	135·599	152·549	169·499	186·449	203·399	220·349	237·299
214	85·147	102·177	119·206	136·236	153·265	170·295	187·324	204·354	221·383	238·413
215	85·545	102·654	119·763	136·872	153·982	171·091	188·200	205·309	222·418	239·527
216	85·943	103·132	120·320	137·509	154·698	171·886	189·075	206·264	223·453	240·641
217	86·341	103·609	120·877	138·146	155·414	172·682	189·950	207·219	224·487	241·755
218	86·739	104·087	121·434	138·782	156·130	173·478	190·826	208·174	225·522	242·869
219	87·137	104·564	121·991	139·419	156·846	174·274	191·701	209·129	226·557	243·983
220	87·534	105·041	122·549	140·055	157·562	175·070	192·577	210·083	227·591	245·098
221	87·932	105·519	123·106	140·692	158·279	175·865	193·452	211·038	228·626	246·212
222	88·330	105·996	123·663	141·329	158·995	176·661	194·327	211·993	229·660	247·326
223	88·728	106·474	124·220	141·965	159·711	177·457	195·203	212·948	230·695	248·440
224	89·126	106·951	124·777	142·602	160·427	178·253	196·078	213·903	231·729	249·554
225	89·524	107·429	125·334	143·239	161·143	179·048	196·953	214·858	232·764	250·668
226	89·922	107·906	125·891	143·875	161·860	179·844	197·829	215·813	233·798	251·782
227	90·320	108·384	126·448	144·512	162·576	180·640	198·704	216·768	234·833	252·896
228	90·718	108·861	127·005	145·148	163·292	181·436	199·579	217·723	235·867	254·010
229	91·115	109·339	127·562	145·785	164·008	182·231	200·455	218·678	236·901	255·124
230	91·513	109·816	128·119	146·422	164·725	183·027	201·330	219·633	237·936	256·238
231	91·911	110·294	128·676	147·058	165·441	183·823	202·205	220·588	238·970	257·352
232	92·309	110·771	129·233	147·695	166·157	184·619	203·081	221·543	240·005	258·467
233	92·707	111·249	129·790	148·332	166·873	185·415	203·956	222·498	241·039	259·581
234	93·105	111·726	130·347	148·968	167·589	186·210	204·831	223·452	242·074	260·695
235	93·503	112·203	130·904	149·605	168·305	187·006	205·707	224·407	243·108	261·809
236	93·901	112·681	131·461	150·241	169·022	187·802	206·582	225·362	244·143	262·923
237	94·299	113·158	132·018	150·878	169·738	188·598	207·457	226·317	245·177	264·037
238	94·696	113·636	132·575	151·515	170·454	189·393	208·333	227·272	246·212	265·151
239	95·094	114·113	133·132	152·151	171·170	190·189	209·208	228·227	247·246	266·265
240	95·492	114·591	133·689	152·788	171·886	190·985	210·084	229·182	248·281	267·379
241	95·890	115·068	134·246	153·424	172·603	191·781	210·959	230·137	249·315	268·493
242	96·288	115·546	134·804	154·061	173·319	192·576	211·834	231·092	250·350	269·607
243	96·686	116·023	135·361	154·698	174·035	193·372	212·710	232·047	251·384	270·721
244	97·084	116·501	135·918	155·334	174·751	194·168	213·585	233·002	252·419	271·835
245	97·482	116·978	136·475	155·971	175·467	194·964	214·460	233·957	253·453	272·950
246	97·879	117·456	137·032	156·607	176·184	195·760	215·336	234·912	254·488	274·064
247	98·277	117·933	137·589	157·244	176·900	196·555	216·211	235·866	255·522	275·178
248	98·675	118·410	138·146	157·881	177·616	197·351	217·086	236·821	256·557	276·292
249	99·073	118·888	138·703	158·517	178·332	198·147	217·962	237·776	257·591	277·406
250	99·471	119·365	139·260	159·154	179·048	198·943	218·837	238·731	258·626	278·520
251	99·869	119·843	139·817	159·790	179·764	199·738	219·712	239·686	259·660	279·634
252	100·267	120·320	140·374	160·427	180·481	200·534	220·588	240·641	260·695	280·748
253	100·665	120·798	140·931	161·064	181·197	201·330	221·463	241·596	261·729	281·862
254	101·063	121·275	141·488	161·701	181·913	202·126	222·338	242·551	262·764	282·976
255	101·461	121·753	142·045	162·337	182·629	202·922	223·214	243·506	263·798	284·090
256	101·858	122·230	142·602	162·974	183·346	203·717	224·089	244·461	264·833	285·204
257	102·256	122·708	143·159	163·610	184·062	204·513	224·964	245·416	265·867	286·319
258	102·654	123·185	143·716	164·247	184·778	205·309	225·840	246·371	266·902	287·433
259	103·052	123·663	144·273	164·884	185·494	206·105	226·715	247·326	267·936	288·547
260	103·450	124·140	144·830	165·520	186·210	206·900	227·591	248·281	268·971	289·661
261	103·848	124·618	145·387	166·157	186·927	207·696	228·466	249·236	270·005	290·775
262	104·246	125·095	145·944	166·793	187·643	208·492	229·341	250·190	271·040	291·889
263	104·644	125·572	146·501	167·430	188·359	209·288	230·217	251·145	272·074	293·003
264	105·041	126·050	147·058	168·067	189·075	210·084	231·092	252·100	273·109	294·117
265	105·439	126·527	147·615	168·703	189·791	210·879	231·967	253·055	274·143	295·231
266	105·837	127·005	148·172	169·340	190·507	211·675	232·843	254·010	275·178	296·345
267	106·235	127·482	148·729	169·977	191·224	212·471	233·718	254·965	276·212	297·459
268	106·633	127·960	149·286	170·613	191·940	213·267	234·593	255·920	277·247	298·573
269	107·031	128·437	149·844	171·250	192·656	214·062	235·469	256·875	278·281	299·687
270	107·429	128·915	150·401	171·886	193·372	214·858	236·344	257·830	279·316	300·802
271	107·827	129·392	150·958	172·523	194·088	215·654	237·219	258·785	280·350	301·916
272	108·225	129·870	151·515	173·160	194·805	216·450	238·095	259·740	281·385	303·030
273	108·622	130·347	152·072	173·796	195·521	217·245	238·970	260·695	282·419	304·144

Table of the Diameters of Wheels, continued.

Number of Teeth.	Pitch. 1¼	Pitch. 1½	Pitch. 1¾	Pitch. 2	Pitch. 2¼	Pitch. 2½	Pitch. 2¾	Pitch. 3	Pitch. 3¼	Pitch. 3½
	Diam.	Diam.	Diam.	Diam.	Diam.	Diam.	Diam.	Diam.	Diam.	Diam.
274	109·020	130·825	152·629	174·433	196·237	218·041	239·845	261·650	283·454	305·258
275	109·418	131·302	153·186	175·069	196·953	218·837	240·721	262·604	284·488	306·372
276	109·816	131·779	153·743	175·706	197·669	219·633	241·596	263·559	285·523	307·486
277	110·214	132·257	154·300	176·343	198·386	220·429	242·471	264·514	286·557	308·600
278	110·612	132·734	154·857	176·979	199·102	221·224	243·347	265·469	287·592	309·714
279	111·010	133·212	155·414	177·616	199·818	222·020	244·222	266·424	288·626	310·828
280	111·408	133·689	155·971	178·253	200·534	222·816	245·098	267·379	289·661	311·942
281	111·806	134·167	156·528	178·889	201·250	223·612	245·973	268·334	290·695	313·057
282	112·203	134·644	157·085	179·526	201·967	224·407	246·848	269·289	291·730	314·171
283	112·601	135·122	157·642	180·162	202·683	225·203	247·724	270·244	292·764	315·285
284	112·999	135·599	158·199	180·799	203·399	225·999	248·599	271·199	293·799	316·399
285	113·397	136·077	158·756	181·436	204·115	226·795	249·474	272·154	294·833	317·513
286	113·795	136·554	159·313	182·072	204·831	227·591	250·350	273·109	295·868	318·627
287	114·193	137·032	159·870	182·709	205·548	228·386	251·225	274·064	296·902	319·741
288	114·591	137·509	160·427	183·346	206·264	229·182	252·100	275·019	297·937	320·855
289	114·989	137·987	160·984	183·982	206·980	229·978	252·974	275·974	298·971	321·969
290	115·387	138·464	161·541	184·619	207·696	230·774	253·851	276·928	300·006	323·083
291	115·784	138·941	162·098	185·255	208·412	231·569	254·726	277·883	301·040	324·197
292	116·182	139·419	162·655	185·892	209·129	232·365	255·602	278·838	302·075	325·311
293	116·580	139·896	163·213	186·529	209·845	233·161	256·477	279·793	303·109	326·426
294	116·978	140·374	163·770	187·165	210·561	233·957	257·352	280·748	304·144	327·540
295	117·376	140·851	164·327	187·802	211·277	234·752	258·228	281·703	305·178	328·654
296	117·774	141·329	164·884	188·438	211·993	235·548	259·103	282·658	306·213	329·768
297	118·172	141·806	165·441	189·075	212·710	236·344	259·978	283·613	307·247	330·882
298	118·570	142·284	165·998	189·712	213·426	237·140	260·854	284·568	308·282	331·996
299	118·967	142·761	166·555	190·348	214·142	237·936	261·729	285·523	309·316	333·110
300	119·365	143·239	167·112	190·985	214·858	238·731	262·605	286·478	310·351	334·224
301	119·763	143·716	167·669	191·622	215·574	239·527	263·480	287·433	311·385	335·338
302	120·161	144·193	168·226	192·258	216·291	240·323	264·355	288·388	312·420	336·452
303	120·559	144·671	168·783	192·895	217·007	241·119	265·231	289·342	313·454	337·566
304	120·957	145·148	169·340	193·531	217·723	241·914	266·106	290·297	314·489	338·680
305	121·355	145·626	169·897	194·168	218·439	242·710	266·981	291·252	315·523	339·794
306	121·753	146·103	170·454	194·805	219·155	243·506	267·857	292·207	316·558	340·909
307	122·151	146·581	171·011	195·441	219·872	244·302	268·732	293·162	317·592	342·027
308	122·548	147·058	171·568	196·078	220·588	245·098	269·607	294·117	318·627	343·133
309	122·946	147·536	172·125	196·714	221·304	245·893	270·483	295·072	319·661	344·251
310	123·344	148·013	172·682	197·351	222·020	246·689	271·358	296·027	320·696	345·365
311	123·742	148·491	173·239	197·988	222·736	247·485	272·233	296·982	321·730	346·479
312	124·140	148·968	173·796	198·624	223·453	248·281	273·109	297·937	322·765	347·593
313	124·538	149·446	174·353	199·261	224·169	249·076	273·984	298·892	323·799	348·707
314	124·936	149·923	174·910	199·898	224·885	249·872	274·859	299·847	324·834	349·821
315	125·334	150·401	175·467	200·534	225·601	250·668	275·735	300·802	325·868	350·935
316	125·732	150·878	176·024	201·171	226·317	251·464	276·610	301·757	326·903	352·049
317	126·129	151·355	176·581	201·807	227·033	252·259	277·485	302·711	327·937	353·163
318	126·527	151·833	177·139	202·444	227·750	253·055	278·361	303·666	328·972	354·278
319	126·925	152·310	177·696	203·081	228·466	253·851	279·236	304·621	330·006	355·392
320	127·323	152·788	178·253	203·717	229·182	254·647	280·112	305·576	331·041	356·506
321	127·721	153·265	178·810	204·354	229·898	255·443	280·987	306·531	332·075	357·620
322	128·119	153·743	179·367	204·991	230·614	256·238	281·862	307·486	333·110	358·734
323	128·517	154·220	179·924	205·627	231·331	257·034	282·738	308·441	334·144	359·848
324	128·915	154·698	180·481	206·264	232·047	257·830	283·613	309·396	335·179	360·962
325	129·313	155·178	181·038	206·900	232·763	258·626	284·488	310·351	336·214	362·076
326	129·710	155·653	181·595	207·537	233·479	259·421	285·364	311·306	337·248	363·190
327	130·108	156·130	182·152	208·174	234·195	260·217	286·239	312·261	338·283	364·304
328	130·506	156·608	182·709	208·810	234·912	261·013	287·114	313·216	339·317	365·418
329	130·904	157·085	183·266	209·447	235·628	261·809	287·990	314·171	340·352	366·532
330	131·302	157·563	183·823	210·083	236·344	262·604	288·865	315·126	341·386	367·647
331	131·700	158·040	184·380	210·720	237·060	263·400	289·740	316·080	342·121	368·761
332	132·098	158·517	184·937	211·357	237·776	264·196	290·616	317·035	343·455	369·875
333	132·496	158·995	185·494	211·993	238·493	264·992	291·491	317·990	344·490	370·989
334	132·894	159·472	186·051	212·630	239·209	265·788	292·366	318·945	345·524	372·103
335	133·291	159·950	186·608	213·267	239·925	266·583	293·242	319·900	346·559	373·217
336	133·689	160·427	187·165	213·903	240·641	267·379	294·117	320·855	347·593	374·331
337	134·087	160·905	187·722	214·540	241·357	268·175	294·992	321·810	348·628	375·445
338	134·485	161·382	188·279	215·176	242·074	268·971	295·868	322·765	349·662	376·559
339	134·883	161·860	188·836	215·813	242·790	269·766	296·743	323·720	350·697	377·673
340	135·281	162·337	189·393	216·450	243·506	270·562	297·619	324·675	351·731	378·787

ART. 49.—The diameter of any other wheel whose pitch is a multiple or measure of the above can (within the tabular number of teeth) be found by multiplication or division. Thus, let the pitch be 7 inches, and the number of teeth 38; then 7 being the double of $3\frac{1}{2}$, under $3\frac{1}{2}$, and opposite 38, will be found 42·335, which being multiplied by 2, gives 84·67 as the diameter required. Or, let the pitch be $\frac{1}{8}$ inch, and the number of teeth 26; then $\frac{1}{8}$ being the sixteenth part of 2 inches, under 2 and opposite 26 will be found 16·552, which, divided by 16, gives 1·0345 as the diameter required.

CHAPTER V.

SPUR WHEELS.

ART. 50.—Having shown the importance of correctly pitching the teeth of wheels, for which rules are given (ART. 45), we shall now direct attention to an illustration of the various parts of a " spur wheel," and afterwards explain the construction of a scale from which the length and thickness of teeth for any pitch can be immediately obtained.

No. 1, Drawing H, represents the boss, one arm, a portion of the rim, and some teeth of a spur wheel. A is the "*eye*" or hole in B the *boss*; C D is the *arm*. This part of a wheel is invariably composed of two pieces, called the *arm*, and the *rib* or *feather*; but, as the two parts are joined together in the form of a cross +, they will, for the sake of clearness, be designated the *face arm* and the *cross arm*; because C is *parallel* to the face of the wheel, and intended to resist the *tangential* strain on the face of the tooth, whereas, D is at *right angles* to, or *across*, the face, and intended to resist the *cross* strain on the wheel; therefore, C is the face arm, and D the cross arm; E is the *web*, intended, when necessary, to strengthen the *rim* F, on the circumference of which are formed the teeth. *a* is the point of the tooth, and *b* the root; *c, e, d* is the pitch line or circle; the curved line from *a* to *c* is called the *face* of the tooth; and the right line, from *c* to *b*, the *flank* of the tooth. N is the *key-way*, cut longitudinally through the boss, in a direct line with one of the arms.

ART. 51.—The *forms* and proportions for the teeth of wheels vary materially with different makers. By *forms*,

the writer means the curvature of the flank and face,
which will be treated of in a future Chapter. The proportions, namely—length, breadth, and thickness may, for
general purposes in mill-work, be taken from the scale
shown at No. 2, Drawing H. In constructing this scale,
the pitch is employed as the most convenient standard of
measure, and is divided into *fifteen* equal parts. The
proportions are preferred to be as follow :—

From pitch line to point of tooth . 5 parts
From pitch line to root of tooth . 6 „
Thickness of tooth . . . . . . 7 „
Width of space between the teeth . 8 „
Thickness of rim of wheel . . . 7½ „

These proportions will be found to agree with the
general practice better than those which recommend
twelve fifteenths for the length of the tooth, and will be
more convenient than the scale composed of *tenths* and
elevenths of the pitch.* But with regard to the space and
thickness of the tooth, attention will be directed to some
required modifications when we come to the practice of
making working drawings. At present we are simply to
consider the subject in a delineative point of view. The
student is therefore required to make a drawing of the
scale, and portion of a wheel illustrating the same, with
which some pains ought to be taken.

ART. 52.—Describe a rectangle A' B' C' D', No. 2,
Drawing H, of any convenient size (say 12 inches ×
3 inches); and draw the diagonal D' B'. Divide B' C' into
fifteen equal parts, and from the fifth, sixth, seventh, and
eighth parts draw lines converging to point D'. If any
line, as *r s*, be now drawn parallel to B' C', such line will
be divided in the same ratio as B' C', and will consequently
represent a scale of *fifteenths*, from which the proportions
of the teeth of a wheel whose pitch is equal to *r s*, can be

---

* *Vide* " Engineer's and Machinist's Assistant," p. 89.

obtained; and so on with any other line drawn in like manner parallel to B′ C′, which, being 3 inches long, is a scale of parts for a wheel of 3 inches pitch. Therefore the triangle B′ D′ C′, with its accompanying lines, will form a scale for the teeth of wheels of any pitch up to 3 inches.

The right line A′ D′ is divided into inches and parts of inches, and the parallel lines drawn therefrom to meet the diagonal B′ D′ are simply indications of the length of the vertical scale lines r s, t u, &c. This line A′ D′ and scale of inches may therefore be dispensed with, except as an exercise in drawing fine, solid, and perfectly even parallel lines to intersect the diagonal in the same point as the *scale* lines. For instance, if A′ D′ be divided into 24 equal parts, and D′ C′ into the same number of equal parts, horizontal lines drawn from A′ D′ ought to intersect the vertical lines drawn from D′ C′ in the diagonal B′ D′: to do this accurately will require much care. The application of the scale and mode of delineating the teeth of a wheel will be explained in the following problem.

PROBLEM XII.

Required the projection of three or more teeth of a wheel of a given pitch and diameter.

ART. 53.—The diameter of the pitch circle represents in all cases the diameter of the wheel. Let the diameter of wheel be 2 feet and pitch $2\frac{7}{8}$ inches. From A as a centre, with a radius of 12 inches, describe the arc c k d, No. 1, Drawing H, which will form a portion of the pitch line for a wheel 2 feet in diameter. From the centre A draw any right line, as A D f. From the scale of fifteenths, which in No. 2 is r s, take 5 parts, and set them off from f to g, No. 1; and from the same scale take 6 parts, from s to 6, and set them off from f to i. With A as a centre,

E

and A i, A g as radii, describe the arcs of two circles to represent the points and roots of the teeth; and from any point d on the pitch line, set off the pitch d k e, equal to the scale line r s. Now the thickness of tooth is 7 parts, therefore make d m equal to 3⅓ parts, and from k, the centre of adjoining tooth, with k m as radius, describe the faces l and m of two adjacent teeth; and proceed in like manner to put in the curves representing the faces of the other teeth, which curves may be continued a short distance within the pitch circle, and joined by radial lines to the rim F, which should be from 7½ to 8 parts in thickness.

In some cases the teeth are strengthened at the root with a " corner-bit," shown at b, which is drawn with a radius of one part or fifteenth; but in delineating wheels of fine pitch these curves are omitted.

ART. 54.—The mode of projecting the teeth of a spur wheel and the construction of a scale for proportioning the teeth having been explained, it may be useful to show how such a scale can be immediately produced should the one above described not be at hand.

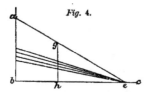

Fig. 4.

Draw two lines a b and b c, Fig. 4, at right angles to each other. With a pair of spring dividers, set off from b, along b a, 15 equal parts of any convenient dimensions. If lines be now drawn from points 5, 6, 7, 8, and 15 to any point, as e, a scale will be at once obtained by drawing g h parallel to a b, and equal in length to the pitch required.

CHAPTER VI.

The Cycloid and other Curves.

BEFORE proceeding with the projection of wheels, it will be desirable to consider the forms and mode of delineating those curves which have been recommended by mathematicians for the flanks and faces of the teeth, namely, the cycloid, epicycloid, hypocycloid, and involute.

The Cycloid.

ART. 55.—The cycloid is a geometrical curve generated by a fixed point in the circumference of a circle, when such circle is caused to roll upon a right line. This is the curve which a nail in the periphery of a carriage wheel describes in the air during one revolution on a level road.

The mode of describing the cycloid is as follows:—

Fig. 5.

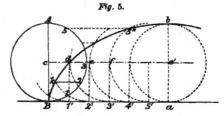

Let A B, Fig. 5, represent the diameter of the generating circle, and B *a* the given right line on which the circle is to roll.   From the centre *c* draw the right line *c c'* parallel

E 2

to B a; then will c c' represent the path or line of motion
of the centre of the circle when rolling along the base line
B a. Divide the semi-circumference of the circle into
any number of equal parts in points 1, 2, 3, &c. Make
B a equal to half the circumference of the generating
circle ($= \dfrac{d\,\pi}{2}$ ART. 41), and divide it into the same number
of equal parts as the semicircle, in points 1′, 2′, 3′, &c.;
then will the right line B 1′ = arc B 1, and B 2′ = arc B 2,
&c. Suppose the circle to be rolled along the line B a
until the centre c arrives at d or e. From point e as a
centre, and with c B as radius, describe a circle; and from
point 2 draw a line parallel to c c', cutting the circle
drawn from e in point k: then will k be one of the points
in the cycloidal curve; and in this manner any number
of points can be obtained. In other words, as the circles,
or portions of the generating circles, are drawn from their
respective centres, set off from point 1′ a segment or
chord equal to B 1; from point 2′ set off a segment
equal to B 2; and so on from the remaining points. Then
draw through these points the curve, which will be the
cycloid required.

ART. 56.—Some of the properties of this curve (on
which depends the doctrine of pendulums) may be interesting. The cycloid is the curve of swiftest descent;
that is to say, a heavy body descending an inverted
cycloid by the force of its own gravity will move from one
point of this curve to another point in less time than it
will take to move in any other curve which *can be drawn
between those points.* Moreover, a body falls through the
arc of an inverted cycloid without acceleration; therefore
the beat of a pendulum, so constructed as to oscillate in
the arc of a cycloid, instead of a circular arc like the
common pendulum, will be perfectly isochronous; that is,
the oscillation will be performed in the same time whether
the arc be large or small. Again, if the generating circle
be placed in the middle of the cycloid, its diameter

coinciding with the cycloidal axis *a b*, Fig. 6, and from any point *c* in the curve A *a* there be drawn the tangent *c e*,

Fig. 6.

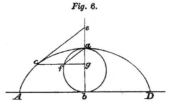

the ordinate *c f g* perpendicular to the axis, and the chord *f a*,—then, *c f* = the circular arc *f a*; the cycloidal arc *a c* = double the chord *a f*; the semi-cycloid *a c* A = double the diameter *a b*; and the tangent *c e* is parallel to the chord *a f*. Further, the area of the whole cycloidal space A *c a* D is equal to three times that of the generating circle *b f a*.

THE EPICYCLOID.

ART. 57.—This curve is generated by a point on the circumference of a circle, which is made to roll upon the outer circumference of a stationary circle.

The construction is as follows, reference being had to No. 1, Drawing I:—Let A B represent the radius of the fixed circle, and A C that of the revolving circle. From B, with the radius B C, describe the arc C C', which will be the path of the centre C, in its motion round the fixed circle. Divide the generating circle into any convenient number of equal parts, in points 1, 2, 3, &c., commencing at A on the line of centres; and from the same point A, set off, along the circumference of the fixed circle, a number of arcs A 1', 1 2', 2 3', &c., each equal in length to the arcs A 1, 1 2, 2 3, &c., of the generator. From B, the centre of large circle, draw the radii B 1', B 2', &c., to cut C C' in points *e, f, g*, &c.; and, from *e, f, g*, as centres, with c A as radius, describe circles, or portions thereof, to represent the successive positions of the generating circle when turning round the fixed circle. If we now suppose the centre c to arrive at e, the arcs or divisions of circles being equal, point 1 will have arrived on the new line of centres B e, and will therefore coincide with 1′; whilst the point A will have arrived at some point k, which is determined by making the arc 1′ k equal to the arc A 1, or by taking B as a centre, with B 1 as radius, and describing a concentric arc from 1 to k, as shown by construction, see point 3 in the generating circle of the epicycloidal curve A e h.

The Hypocycloid.

ART. 58.—The construction of this curve, which is produced by a fixed point in a circle that rolls along the *concave* side of the circumference of a fixed circle, is so nearly allied to the construction of the epicycloid, that a transposition of the letters of reference from No. 1 to No. 2, with the foregoing description, will be sufficient to explain the mode of describing the hypocycloid.

ART. 59.—When constructing the hypocycloid it should be remembered that, if the diameter of the rolling circle is equal to the radius of the quiescent circle, as shown at No. 3, the line described by a fixed point in the rolling circle B n o, will be a perfectly right line bisecting the fixed circle. For instance, a fixed point at B, in the revolving circle B n o, would describe the right line A A′; and in like manner, a fixed point at n would describe the right line n m. This peculiarity in the motion of a fixed point in a revolving circle, whose diameter is equal to the radius of the quiescent circle, has suggested a very simple mode of converting a rotary motion into a rectilinear one, and the converse, by what is called " White's parallel motion," or the " epicycloidal wheel," which we shall have occasion to notice hereafter.

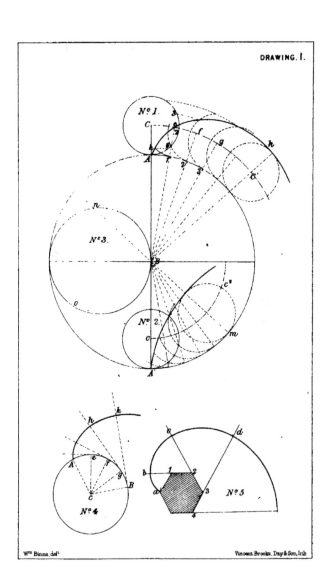

The Involute.

ART. 60.—This curve is produced by the unwinding of a thread from a solid of any given form; which form is called the *evolute*.　A great many curves may be generated in this manner, but that which is more immediately connected with our subject is the involute of the circle.

Let A B, No. 4, Drawing I, represent a circle, around which is wound a piece of thread with a pencil attached at any point A.　If the thread be kept in a state of tension and unwrapped, the pencil will describe the involute curve A *h k*.　This curve may be drawn in the following manner:—From A set off along the circle any number of equal parts *e, f, g*, B, and draw the radial lines *e c, f c*, &c.　From points *e, f, g*, B, draw lines perpendicular to the radials.　These lines being tangents to the circle, and made equal in length to the respective arcs A *e*, A *f*, A *g*, &c., will represent the string in various positions, and the points through which the curve A *h k* is drawn.

ART. 61.—If the evolute be a hexagon, the involute may be obtained as follows:—Let the sides of the hexagon 4 3, 3 2, 2 1, No. 5, Drawing I, be extended indefinitely by right lines, which will represent the string in those positions.　Now, during the process of unwinding, the end of the string, which is at *a*, will first describe the arc *a b*, from point 1 as a centre; the string will then move on point 2 as a centre and describe the arc *b c*; next, from point 3, it will describe the arc *c d*; and so on to any extent. The application of these curves to the teeth of wheels will be referred to hereafter.

CHAPTER VII.

The Delineation of Spur Wheels.

Before we proceed to explain the application of the foregoing curves to the teeth of wheels, and the mode adopted by millwrights for "striking out" the teeth, we must request the student to follow us through the projection of a pair of spur wheels working together, commonly called "in gear."

Problem XIII.

To divide a given circle into any number of equal parts.

Art. 62.—Let the diameter of the circle be $6\frac{1}{4}$ inches, and the number of equal parts or divisions for the centres of the teeth forty-two. The first thing is to find a divisor or measure of the number of equal parts, which in this case is 6, as $6 \times 7 = 42$. If the circumference be now accurately divided into six equal parts, and each of those parts subdivided into seven equal parts, the work will be done. To do it properly, however, requires care; for it will not be considered satisfactory if more than 42 punctures or centres are visible on the surface of the paper; and those centres or divisions must be equidistant, otherwise some of the teeth and spaces will be unequal. To accomplish this and avoid filling the paper with holes, a little practice and attention to the following remarks will be necessary.

Commence the first divisions, whether six or any other number, with a pair of sharp-pointed compasses, or spring dividers, taking care to place the point, at each step, in the *centre of the pencil line,* and especially not to press on the instrument (its weight being sufficient) until you have got the correct extent of opening for each division, when a small puncture must be made with the leg of the compasses *in a vertical position.*

The subdivisions may now be determined in like manner, care being taken not to make indents in the paper, however small, until the proper distance, by trial, has been obtained, when the punctures must be made with the leg of the dividers in a vertical position, as shown by Fig. 7, which will ensure a perpendicular centre-point for striking the curves of the teeth in the manner already explained (ART. 53). If the puncture be made with one leg, before the other has been removed from the paper, as shown in Fig. 8, we not only get an oblique centre-point, but the angular position of the legs tends, by deflection, to open the dividers and to increase the space between the two points. Although this measure is exceedingly small in one division, the error becomes disagreeably large when the circle has to be " stepped " all round, as would be the case if the divisions were 41, or any other number of which a divisor or measure could not be found. To the draughtsman these remarks (which also apply to dividing a right line) may appear simple; they are necessary, however, and if attended to, will prevent many failures.

Fig. 7.

Fig. 8.

ART. 63.—Having divided the circle into 42 equal

parts, proceed, as directed (ART. 53), to draw three concentric circles, representing the points and roots of the teeth and the rim of the wheel, taking 5 parts from pitch line to point, 6 parts from pitch line to root, and 8 parts for the thickness of the rim. Now, if the pitch circle be 6·634, that is very nearly 6¾ inches diameter, the pitch of the teeth will be ½ inch; therefore, from the ½ inch scale (No. 2, Drawing H), take the half of seven parts, the thickness of tooth, and proceed to put in the teeth, as already described, except the "corner-bits" at the root, which may be omitted (ART. 53), the radial lines, or flanks of the teeth, being drawn to touch the root circle.

ART. 64.—In order to make a good drawing, the student must avoid perforating the sheet of paper with the point of his compasses in the centre of the wheel; otherwise he will find it difficult to put in the points and roots of the teeth satisfactorily. When a number of concentric circles have to be drawn, first in pencil and then in ink, it is desirable to try how many of those circles can be made without perforating the paper. This caution is deemed necessary, as the writer has seen so many failures from the leg of the compass penetrating the drawing board to an extent which rendered it impossible to make a satisfactory drawing without recommencing the work a second and sometimes a third time. To avoid this difficulty it has been proposed to make use of a transparent horn disc with a small puncture in the centre, and three small pins to *stick into and deface the paper;* but with ordinary care the work can be done better without this appliance.

Having delineated the rim and teeth in pencil, proceed to draw the several parts in ink, commencing with the concentric circles of the boss and faces of the teeth (ART. 7), and afterwards drawing the flanks. For this purpose a very fine needle may be inserted in the centre of the wheel, to form an axis or guide for the " set square " to rest against, which will greatly facilitate the operation of drawing in the flanks or radial lines of the teeth.

ART. 65.—The student may now proceed to represent another wheel " in gear " with the one just described ; the second wheel to be 5·092, say $5\frac{1}{10}$ inches diameter, and have 32 teeth, the divisor or measure of which is 4, as $4 \times 8 = 32$. Draw the right line $s\ t$, Fig. 9, which is

Fig. 9.

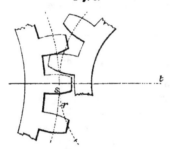

called *the line of centres.* From s, the pitch line of large wheel, set off $s\ t$ equal to the radius 2·55 inches of small wheel ; and from t, the centre, describe the pitch circle, *which must always touch the pitch circle of the wheel with which it is in gear.*

ART. 66.—To avoid a common mistake of dividing the pitch circle of the second wheel in such manner that its teeth will not fit into the spaces of the first wheel, set off from the face of that tooth nearest the line of centres half the thickness of a tooth, as $r\ s$, Fig. 9 : then will r be the centre of the first tooth, and the point whence the divisions may be commenced, in order to ensure accuracy in the disposition of the teeth, which must be represented in gear, as shown in Fig. 9.

ART. 67.—When it is required to delineate the teeth of wheels on a small scale, much time may be saved, after the pitch line has been accurately divided, by setting off

the pitch circle and pitch on a separate piece of paper, as
shown in Fig. 10, and finding, by trial, a radius which

Fig. 10.

will describe the face and flank of tooth
at one stroke of the bow pen. The
"spring bow" being thus set, and the
concentric circles for the pitch line,
point, and root drawn in pencil, the
whole of the teeth can at once be
described with ink, thus avoiding the
necessity of pencilling in the flanks and faces.

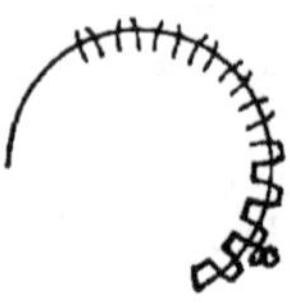

Edge View of a Wheel.

Art. 68.—If the edge view of a wheel be correctly
delineated, the centre tooth, as *s*, Fig. 9, will be represented by four lines, *i.e.* two from the point and two
from the thick part on the pitch line; whereas the teeth
adjoining will be represented by three lines, *i.e.* two from
the point and one from the root; whilst others will be
represented by two lines only. To avoid this confusion
of lines it is usual, in outline drawings, to represent each
tooth with only two lines; the first being drawn from the
upper or lower angle of the point of tooth, and the second
from some point situated between the point and pitch line,
so as to make the gradations of the teeth and spaces
uniform and consequently more pleasing. See edge view
of spur wheel B, Drawing O.

Boss and Key-ways.

Art. 69.—The boss or centre part of a wheel is generally bored out, and the shaft accurately turned to fit it;
in which case one key, with a sunk key-way in the shaft,
or a flat bed planed on the shaft, are the usual means for

securing the wheel in its place. For heavy work, such as the boss of a paddle wheel or water wheel, three keys at equal angles are employed, the key-ways being sunk both in the boss and shaft, and to the same depth in each. When the *eye* of the boss is cast larger than the shaft, four keys are used at equal angles, with corresponding flats planed on the shaft; a mode of fixing which is also adopted with

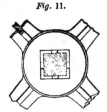

Fig. 11.

square shafts, as shown by Fig. 11, in which eight keys, namely, one at each corner of the shaft, are employed when necessary.

* * *

KEYS.

ART. 70.—When one key is employed, its breadth should not be less than $\frac{1}{8}$th of the diameter of the shaft; thickness, $\frac{3}{4}$ths of the breadth; and taper, for large shafts, $\frac{1}{8}$th of an inch in 18 inches. When three keys are used, the breadth is $\frac{1}{8}$th or $\frac{1}{7}$th of the diameter of shaft; and thickness $\frac{1}{2}$ths of the breadth.

ART. 71.--For the strength of the boss, it is stated in a modern work,* that " a thickness of 5 inches may be considered a maximum for the bosses of moderately sized wheels;" but the student is not told what is meant by " moderately sized." A 4-feet wheel, $1\frac{1}{4}$ inch pitch, on a 4-inch shaft, would be considered " moderately sized "; but a boss " 5 inches " thick, or 14 inches in diameter, on the same wheel or shaft, would be anything but moderate. Such statements being calculated to mislead the student, the writer would remark that the rule for the thickness of

---

* *Vide,* "The Practical Draughtsman's Book of Industrial Design," p. 77.

the boss is simply that it is usually made equal to the pitch. That is to say, in wheels of 3 inches pitch, for ordinary mill gearing, the boss is 3 inches thick; for 2 inches pitch, the boss is 2 inches thick; and so on for any other pitch, except in wheels for rolling mills and similar work, where the gearing is subject to heavy shocks and strains, that require great additional strength, not only in the boss, but also in the arms.

ARMS OF WHEELS.

ART. 72.—Although wheels are very rarely made with five arms, there is no reasonable objection to that number; therefore,

Wheels from 1¼ ft. to 3 ft. diameter may have 4 arms

,,	,,	3	,,	5	,,	,,	5	,,
,,	,,	5	,,	8	,,	,,	6	,,
,,	,,	8	,,	16	,,	,,	8	,,

Wheels of less diameter than 15 or 18 inches are generally made without arms, the rim being connected to the boss by a web or plate; and when so constructed they are called *plate wheels*. The arms of spur wheels are in the form of a +, and those of bevel wheels in the form of a T, as will be hereafter explained.

STRENGTH OF WHEEL ARMS.

ART. 73.—The strength which it is considered necessary to make the arms of wheels is more a matter of opinion than one of rule, and, after looking at the formula contained in a treatise on the strength of cast iron now before us, we are not surprised at millwrights being guided entirely by their own judgment, referring, in cases of doubt, to other patterns of similar size, and from their appearance deciding on the proportions to be given to the work in hand.   Students, however, seldom have patterns or wheels to look at, and therefore require some simple kind of rule or scale to assist them in delineating the arms of wheels.

ART. 74.—Adopting the pitch as a standard of measure and index of the strength of a toothed wheel, we proceed to take the dimensions of arms, &c., from the scale of fifteenths, reference being had to No. 1, Drawing K, which represents a portion of a spur wheel of 9 feet diameter and 3 inches pitch, with eight arms, drawn to a scale of an inch to the foot, the proportions of the arms being given in fifteenths of the pitch.

Fifteenths.

Depth $a\ b$ of face arm at the rim   . $=$ 25
      The depth to increase ½ an inch for every foot in length as it approaches the boss, and ¼ of an inch when the wheels have four arms.

Breadth $c\ d$ of face arm   .   . $=$ 6
      and to be parallel throughout its entire length.

Depth or thickness $i\ k$ of cross arm where it joins the rim   .   .   .   . $=$ 5

Depth or thickness of cross arm at the boss   .   .   .   .   .   . $=$ 6

Breadth $e\ f$ of cross arm at the rim to be 12 parts *less* than the breadth $g\ h$ of wheel.

Breadth $l\ m$ of cross arm at the boss to equal the breadth of wheel.

Thickness $l\ n$ of boss   .   .   . $=$ 15 to 17

Thickness of rim   .   .   .   . $=$ 7 to 8

To render the illustration on Drawing K more useful, we have marked the number of fifteenths of the pitch opposite each member of the wheel, and would recommend

the student to make a drawing of portions of three or
more wheels, say 4, 6, and 8 feet in diameter, and of
different pitches.

Although the above proportions are nearly double those
obtained by the formula given in the fourth edition of
Tredgold "On the Strength of Cast-Iron," p. 216, they
are less than we sometimes find them in practice. They
will serve the purpose of the student, however, and for
ordinary gearing will be found to bear a strain much
greater than that which would fracture the cogs, as will
be evident from the following explanation.

ART. 75.—Taking Mr. Fairbairn's estimate of the
strength of an inch bar of Low Moor iron to be 2,124 lbs.,
and the arm, as a cantilever, fixed at one end and loaded
at the other, or as bearing ¼th the weight of a beam
supported at both ends and loaded in the middle, we get

$$\frac{2124 \times t \times d^2}{L} = 25832, \text{ and } 25832 \div 4 = 6458$$

as the ultimate strength of one arm, in which t is the
breadth or thickness = 1·25 inch, d the depth = 6 inches,
and L the length = 3·7 feet.

Again, if we take the working load at $\frac{1}{10}$th of the
ultimate strength, and the number of arms as 8, we have

$$\frac{6458 \times 8}{10} = 5166·4 \text{ lbs.}$$

for the safe load of all the arms combined, which is
approximately equal to a power of 132 horses, supposing
the wheel No. 1, Drawing K, to make 30 revolutions per
minute.

In machinery for rolling, punching, and shearing metal,
and in cases where the wheel has to drive two or more
pinions, a greater strength of arm will be necessary; *
but the impossibility of laying down a rule or formula for

* Since writing the above, the Author has been favoured with a copy
of a "Practical Treatise on Mill Gearing," by Mr. Thomas Box, which,
in addition to much useful matter, contains reliable formulæ on the
strength of wheel-arms. Published by Messrs. E. & F. N. Spon.

shocks and vibrations suggests the importance of recommending the student to careful observation in the workshop, and especially to note all cases of failure and of fractures with which he may meet; he should also devote particular attention to the practice of making to scale drawings of first-class machinery, which, so to speak, will educate the eye and accustom it to the proportions of parts of machines to which machine makers never think of applying a rule. It is necessary to caution the student, however, against placing too much reliance on this kind of practice, although more machines have been made by it than by any other; and here it may not be out of place to relate an anecdote that will in some measure illustrate the manner in which many of our machines are constructed, and show the importance of acquiring a knowledge of the principles of mechanics and the strength of materials.

ART. 76.—Many years since, the writer was greatly interested in watching the operations of the leading hands in a celebrated firm, who were then engaged in making a machine for perforating sheets of tin. 500 holes, about $\frac{1}{4}$ inch diameter, were intended to be punched in each sheet at one operation. For this purpose, a rectangular plate of steel, drilled with the required number of holes, and a corresponding plate with the same number of steel punches were accurately fitted and placed between two cast-iron standards, connected by a wrought-iron crosshead, through which passed a screw, about $1\frac{1}{2}$ inch diameter, to act on the punch-plate, with a lever some 3 feet long for giving motion to the same. This really admirable piece of workmanship being completed, it was decided to try the effect of simultaneously punching 500 holes through a sheet of *brown paper*; the result, however, was a permanent set or bending of the hand-lever, followed by fracture of the standards, creating no little surprise amongst those who witnessed the first trial and failure, which was followed by many others before the machine was finished.

F

Now, in this case a knowledge of the elementary principles was peculiarly applicable, and could have been brought to bear in such a manner as at once to determine the pitch of screw (which is a modification of the inclined plane), the length of lever, and the force to be applied. If, for instance, a single punch had been " rigged up" with a lever, the force required to punch one hole would have been ascertained; and that force multiplied by 500 would have given some idea of the maximum power that would be required to do the work. Such expedients, however, were never thought of, and it was not until the machine had been constructed and reconstructed three or four times, that half the number of holes (250) could be simultaneously punched through a sheet of tin! On the other hand, we have all the particulars of a machine, wherein the actual amount of work done was less than one-eighth of that which had previously been estimated by several profound mathematicians.

ART. 77.—Of all the patented machines, those for " obtaining and applying motive power" exhibit, as a rule, the most lamentable amount of ignorance of elementary principles on the part of their promoters. Let the reader imagine a truck or frame (see Fig. 12), mounted on six wheels, and carrying two large wedge-shaped boxes or vessels (reversed on the carriage frame), as well as an air-pump, for exhausting the air from one or other of the said vessels, and he will realize the principle of a patented would-be-motive-power-machine which, after the air had been pumped out from one of the vessels, was to be propelled by the external pressure of the atmosphere (14·75 lbs. per square inch—say, for a partial vacuum, 10 lbs. per square inch) on the head of the wedge-shaped vessel, thus— This diagram may be said to represent the carriage and lower vessel, the upper vessel (not shown) being exhausted of air when it was desired to

Fig. 12.

reverse the motion of the machine. It is stated in the specification, that the sides of the vessels being equal, the pressures will balance each other; that the atmospheric pressure on the under side *will be counteracted by the gravity of the carriage*; but that the area of one end being 1000 square inches in excess of the other end, the result will be a propelling power of $1000 \times 10 = 10,000$ lbs.

These examples have been introduced with a view of impressing upon the student the importance of combining with his practice in the workshop a knowledge of the principles of mechanics, hydraulics, hydrostatics, and pneumatics, treatises on which may now be had in a very cheap form.

CHAPTER VIII.

Mortise and other Wheels.

Art. 78.—A *mortise* is a cavity cut in a piece of wood or other material, to receive a corresponding piece called a *tenon*, which may be formed of another piece of wood; hence the term " mortise," as applied to a wheel of the following description:—A A′, Fig. 13, represents the front elevation, and B B the plan or edge view of a portion of the rim of one of these wheels, in which is cast a

Fig. 13.

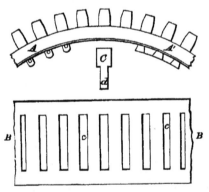

number of mortise holes *c c*; and into these holes is accurately fitted the slightly tapered tenon *d* of the rough cog C *d*. These wooden *cogs*, as they are now called, are generally made of good dry mountain beech, hornbeam, or hickory ; and being tightly driven into the mortise holes, are then firmly secured by driving wrought-iron pins longitudinally through the shanks, as shown at A. Sometimes the ends of the cogs are dovetailed, and a dovetail key of the same kind of wood driven between each pair of shanks, as shown at A'. The former plan is generally preferred on account of cost, and the liability of wooden keys to get loose by shrinking. The cogs having been firmly fixed, as described, the wheel is then turned true on the face, and the cogs reduced to the proper shape by means of a revolving cutter or by hand.

DRIVER AND FOLLOWER.

ART. 79.—The first motion wheel of a train is called the *driver*; and the second motion wheel, with which it is in gear, is called the *follower*. Now a mortise wheel is generally, but not necessarily, the driver; and the object of employing wooden teeth is to prevent the noise and vibration which occur with wheels running at high velocities, when the teeth are iron working against iron. This kind of wheel is therefore extensively used for giving motion to the " nut," or pinion, on the end of the spindle of mill-stones, and in other cases where great speeds are required.

ART. 80.—The amount of *stepping*, as it were, of one tooth upon another, when a pair of wheels are in action, will depend upon the pitch. In rolling contact, where the teeth are microscopic and innumerable, it is nothing, because the action takes place at the point of contact, which is on the line of centres; but, in properly constructed toothed wheels, the action of one tooth upon another commences at a distance from the line of centres equal to about half the pitch, consequently the *stepping* motion will increase in the same ratio as the pitch. In the case of a planing machine, the table of which was driven by a rack * and pinion, where the mark of every tooth, or step, was left by the tool on the planed metal surface, recourse was had to Dr. Hooke's gearing, a description of which was submitted to the Royal Society in 1666 as " the perfection of wheel work."

DR. HOOKE'S GEARING.

ART. 81.—This form of gearing consists in bolting together, face to face, a number of plate (or armed) wheels of the same pitch, and in such manner that the teeth of each wheel are in advance of the teeth of the

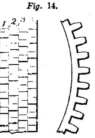

Fig. 14.

next adjoining wheel, as shown by 1, 2, 3, 4 in Fig. 14, which represents a face view of one wheel, and an edge view of a group of wheels combined on Dr. Hooke's principle. Thus, let there be four wheels, of any given breadth on the face, and 2 inches pitch, bolted together in such order that the teeth of the second wheel are in advance of the first one-fourth of the pitch, and so on with the third and fourth wheels of the group; the pinion being constructed in the same manner, it will be obvious that the number of *steps*, or *contacts*, will be four times that of an ordinary wheel of the same pitch; consequently the inequalities of motion will be reduced three-fourths. In other terms, we get the strength of a wheel equal to 2 inches pitch with the smoothness of action that would

---

* A straight bar with teeth on one of its sides, equivalent to a wheel of infinite radius.

attend the working of a pair of wheels of $\frac{1}{2}$ inch pitch
The greatest effect would be obtained by filing off the
corners of the teeth diagonally, see Fig. 15, *Fig.* 15.
which represents an edge view of a wheel and
pinion of this kind. The action of the teeth
in this case, if properly formed, would be
always on the line of centres, but attended with
an end thrust on the line of shaft, which, in
heavy gearing, would be objectionable.

The writer has seen Dr. Hooke's gearing
employed for driving the propeller of a screw
boat, where smoothness of action is so desirable; but he does not remember an application
of it in mill-gearing, probably on account of its first
cost.

FRICTIONAL GEARING.

ART. 82.—This is a form of wheel which has been
known to produce most brilliant pyrotechnic effects, by
the slipping and grinding of surfaces when the weight was
suddenly thrown on. It is termed " Robertson's patent
wedge and grooved frictional gear-   *Fig.* 16.
ing," and said to be " advanta-
geously applicable to the heaviest
as well as the lightest kinds of
machine and millwright work, and
especially so when the speeds are
high, and where it is of importance
to avoid noise, backlash, or risk
of breakage." A front and edge
view of a pair of these wheels are
given in Fig. 16, where in place
of projecting teeth, as before described, the peripheries
of the wheels are made with a series of V projections,

which fit into corresponding grooves of the pinion, so
that A may drive B by the friction of contact or "bite"
of the V's and wedges. There is no doubt that wheels
of this kind will work very smoothly where the power
transmitted is slight, the velocity tolerably high, and
the wheels perfectly true; but, like the driving wheels
of a locomotive in starting, they are liable to slip and
give out sparks of fire, which in many cases would be
attended with danger. It will also be observed, that in
all points of contact the pressure is in the direction of
the line of centres; and this is objectionable on account of
friction, which increases with the weight.

ANTI-FRICTION WHEELS.

ART. 83.—A side elevation and plan of this arrangement of wheels for reducing the velocity of rubbing
surfaces is shown at Fig. 17. By
allowing each end of an axis $c\ c'$
to rest upon the peripheries of
two plain wheels $a'\ b'$, $a\ b$, the
friction of the principal bearings
$c'\ c$, which roll upon the circumferences of the four wheels, is
transmitted to eight pivots, whose
motion is very slow compared
with the axis $c'\ c$. As examples of
the employment of anti-friction
wheels, it may be mentioned that
they have been applied to the axes
of grindstones, as also to the more
delicate machine invented by Mr. Attwood, for experi-
menting on the accelerated motion of falling bodies.

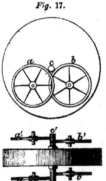

Fig. 17.

CARRIER AND CHANGE WHEELS.

ART. 84.—When two shafts, revolving in the same direction, lie so close together that the wheels must be placed side by side, the mode of communicating motion from one shaft to the other is by a *carrier wheel*. Fig. 18 represents a plan and elevation of this carrier-wheel arrangement, in which b', the driver, gives motion through A, the carrier, to c', the follower, which moves in the same direction as b', as indicated by the arrows. It can also be shown that c' and b' move with the same velocity ratio as if those two wheels were in gear with each other. Fig. 19 repre-

Fig. 18.

sents a transverse section of a set of drawing rollers employed in spinning machinery, in which the circumferential velocity of the front pair of rollers a is required to be greater than that of the middle pair b, and of b to be greater than the velocity of the back rollers c, so as to draw

Fig. 19.

out the fibres, and thereby elongate the "sliver" or cotton cord $e\ f$. In this case the carrier is generally employed in transmitting motion from the middle pair of rollers to the back pair; and in order that the velocity ratio of all the pairs may be altered to spin a fine or coarse thread, by a greater or less attenuation of the fibres, recourse is had to a system of gearing called *change wheels*, consisting of a number of small wheels and pinions of various sizes that are made to fit the ends of the bottom rollers, and also an intermediate axis, not shown in the engraving. By this gearing the velocity ratio of the set of rollers can be changed at pleasure; hence the name of "change wheels," in all probability first given to this system of gearing, which is also employed in the screw-cutting lathe.

NOTE.—The wheel A, Fig. 18, is by many writers called a *Marlborough* or *idle* wheel; but as we cannot see how a thing can be idle when it works, we prefer the more general nomenclature of *carrier* wheel.

INTERMEDIATE WHEEL.

ART. 85.—This is simply another application of the carrier wheel (see A, Fig. 20) placed between two others

Fig. 20.

(B and C) for the purpose of transmitting motion from one axis to another without change of direction. If B and C were in contact, they would revolve in opposite directions; but in consequence of the use of the intermediate or carrier wheel A (also erroneously called an *idle* wheel) they revolve in the same direction, and without any change in the velocity ratio of the pair.

ECCENTRIC AND ELLIPTICAL WHEELS.

ART. 86.—Spur wheels are often employed for other purposes than that of producing simple rotary motion. When the velocity ratio of the *driver* is constant, and

Fig. 21.

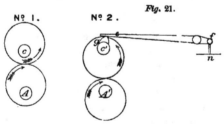

a variable velocity ratio is required in the *follower*, a pair of eccentric wheels may be employed, as at Fig. 21,

which represents the pitch lines of a pair of such
wheels in extreme positions. A A′ being the axis of
the driver, and c c′ the axis of the follower, it is manifest
that the velocity ratio of c, when in position No. 1, will
be at its maximum, and when in position No.
2 at its
minimum. This gradually accelerated and retarded
motion of the follower has been employed by Messrs.
Maudslay, Sons, & Field for punching thin boiler plates.
Thus, a lever, e f, actuated by a cam, g, on the shaft c
(No. 2), gives motion to a punch,

Fig. 22.

n. It will therefore be seen
that advantage is taken of the
greatest amount of power exerted
by the driver A′, and consequently the least velocity of the
follower, for driving the punch
through the plate.

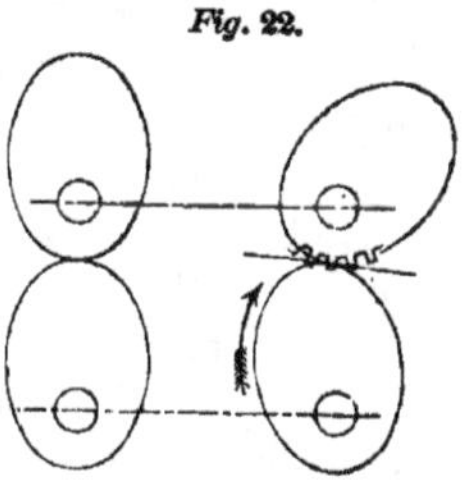

ART. 87.—Fig. 22 represents
the pitch lines of a pair of elliptical wheels in two positions, of which it is only necessary to remark that the
projection of the teeth in such
wheels will be perpendicular
to the tangential line drawn
through the point of contact.
In this arrangement, also, we
have a retarded and accelerated
motion of the axis of the follower, produced by a uniform
motion of the axis of the driver.

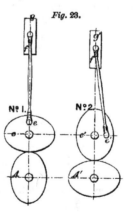

Fig. 23.

Nº 1.　　Nº 2.

ART. 88.—Fig. 23 repre-
sents a pair of elliptical wheels
with the axis in the centre
of each ellipse. The object
sought to be attained by this
arrangement is to convert a
constant rotary motion into a reciprocating, and at the
same time uniform, rectilinear motion with one pair of

wheels. The most simple mode of converting rotary into rectilinear motion is by means of a crank or a stud in the face of a wheel, with a connecting rod attached thereto; a mode generally adopted in " shaping " and " slotting " machines, for giving motion to an arm or bar of iron that carries the cutting tool. The motion in this case, however, like that of the piston of a steam engine, is a variable one, and therefore not applicable for moving the table of what is called a " drill slotting," or rather metal mortising, machine, which requires the table to travel to and fro with uniform velocity. For this purpose we have seen employed a pair of elliptical wheels with the axis in the centre of each ellipse, as at Fig. 23, in which the pitch lines of the wheels are represented in two positions. In the face of the follower c is fixed a stud or crank pin e, which carries the end of a connecting rod $e\ f$. Therefore when the crank pin is at what is called the " dead point " (see No. 1), the upper ellipse or follower is moving at its greatest velocity; and when the pin is at " half stroke " (which is the greatest velocity of a piston) the follower c' (No. 2), is moving at its least velocity; and this accelerated and retarded rotary motion of the crank pin produces a uniform rectilinear motion of the slide or table $g\ g'$.

MANGLE WHEEL.

ART. 89.—This term is applied to a combination of toothed wheels, whereby a continuous rotary motion of the driver is made to produce a periodical change in the direction of motion of the follower.

When the teeth of a pinion act upon the teeth of an ordinary spur wheel, the two axes turn in opposite directions; but when they act on the teeth of an *internal* wheel

(ART. 90), the two axes revolve in the same direction; and so, by combining a spur wheel with an *internal* wheel, a *mangle wheel* is produced.

These wheels vary in their construction, but those we have seen employed in "slubbing" and "roving" frames were of the form shown at Fig. 24, in which No. 1 is a

Fig. 24.

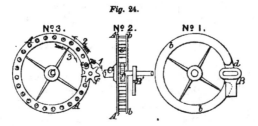

side elevation, No. 2 an edge view, and No. 3 a section, showing the front plate *b b* removed.

The wheel consists of an annular plate A A, No. 3, mounted on an axis C C, and an annular plate *b b*, cast in one piece, with projecting *staves* or teeth *e e'*, leaving an interval or gap at *d* for the passage of the pinion *f* to and from the inside of the wheel in the following manner :— The axis of the pinion has a lateral or pendulous motion, governed by a slot plate, shown in position at B B'. Now suppose the pinion to have a right-hand motion, as indicated by the arrow 1, it would, with its axis at the right-hand end of slot plate B, drive the wheel in an *opposite direction*, as indicated by arrow 2; but, by continuing the motion of the pinion, the tooth *e*, with which it is in contact, will act upon the tooth of the pinion in such manner as to cause the axis of the pinion to move from the right-hand end of the slot to the left, thereby carrying the pinion through the gap: in which position it would commence driving the internal wheel in the *same direction* as itself, as indicated by the arrow 3, and would continue to do so until the interval *d* again came opposite the slot plate, when the pinion would leave the internal wheel and re-commence driving the external wheel.*

ANNULAR WHEEL.

ART. 90.—An annular wheel is one having its teeth formed within its periphery, and consequently the pinion works internally : hence the more common name of *internal wheel.*

ART. 91.—It has been shown (ART. 59) that when the diameter of the generating circle is equal to the radius of the internal wheel, a fixed point in the generatrix will describe a right line, a property which has suggested another method of converting rotary into rectilinear motion, by what is called the epicycloidal or hypocycloidal train. An example of this is shown at Fig. 25, in which

Fig. 25.

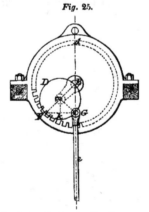

the internal wheel A F is firmly fixed concentrically with a driving shaft B, on the end whereof is keyed a crank B *c*,

---

* Although Fig. 24 is sufficient to explain the action of this mechanical contrivance, there are errors in the above projections of the figures, which errors will serve as an exercise for the student to correct in his drawing of the mangle wheel.

shown in dotted lines. Now the shaft B and crank arm being made to revolve and carry with them the pinion D, which runs loosely on the crank pin c, the pump or other rod G e—attached to the pinion by a stud, whose centre is in the pitch line of the pinion and coincident with the vertical diameter of the wheel—will move in the right line G e; and a parallel motion will be thus obtained. This elegant, though not particularly useful, motion was originally proposed by Mr. Murray, of the firm of Messrs. Fenton and Murray, Leeds, but is known as White's parallel motion, from its having been published by that gentleman in his work entitled " Century of Inventions "

ART. 92.—The following geometrical proof that point G will describe the right line G A may not be uninteresting:—Draw B F passing through c, and G F to meet F in the point of contact of the two pitch circles; on G F let fall perpendicular c k. Now, since an angle at the centre c is double the angle at the circumference, we have B c G $= 2$ B F G, and B $= 2$ cos c B G; but the length of the arcs which these angles subtend, when multiplied by their radii, are equal; hence the angle of the larger circumference being half that of the smaller, but its radius double the radius of the smaller, the arcs subtended by these angles are themselves equal, and therefore, in all positions, the point G will be found in the vertical line G A; and since B G $= 2$ cos c B G, the velocity ratio of G to c B will be the same as the common crank, and the motion produced in G equal to that which would be given by a crank with a radius equal to 2 c B, the connecting rod being supposed of indefinite length.

ART. 93.—Internal wheels are variously employed, and especially for transmitting power from water wheels. For this purpose they are cast in segments, and bolted to the " shrouding," i.e. the side plates that carry the buckets. The Greenock water wheel, erected by Mr. James Smith of Deanston (an admirable piece of work), is 69 feet 6 inches in diameter, with an annular wheel of 67 feet 6 inches diameter, which is the largest with which we are acquainted.

CHAPTER IX.

TEETH OF WHEELS IN PRACTICE.

ART. 94.—In describing the faces of the teeth of an annular wheel and pinion, *intended to work together*, two generating circles are recommended to be employed; one for the faces of the wheel teeth, and the other for the faces of the teeth of pinion, *the flanks in both cases being radial lines.* See No. 2, Drawing K.

ART. 95.—Now, the curve for the faces of the teeth of the wheel is obtained by rolling (ART. 58), on the *inside* of the pitch circle of the wheel, a circle whose *diameter* is equal to the *radius of the pinion*; and the curve for the teeth of the pinion is obtained by rolling, *outside* the pitch circle of the pinion, a circle whose *diameter* is equal to the *radius of the wheel.* But supposing it were required to take the power from two opposite points in the circumference of an internal driving wheel by two pinions of different radii, it is manifest that the teeth of the three wheels could not be perfectly formed as above described, and that some modification, similar to that employed in the construction of spur wheels, would be necessary. Before entering on this part of our subject, however, it is desirable the student should work out the following exercise in the practical construction of teeth, according to ARTS. 57 and 58.

Problem XIV.

*Required the projection of a segment of an internal wheel
and a pinion to work in the same: the diameter of wheel to
be 120·32 inches, with 108 teeth; and the diameter of
pinion 24·51 inches, with 22 teeth; the pitch being 3½
inches. Scale 1½ inch to 1 foot.*

Art. 96.—From any point A, No. 2, Drawing K, as a
centre, and with A B as radius, draw the pitch line B D of
wheel. And from C as centre, with C B as radius, describe the pitch line B E of pinion. Proceed to find the
hypocycloidal curve B ƒ for the face of the teeth of wheel,
by rolling the circle B g along the pitch circle D B of the
wheel, as already described. Set off the pitch and thickness of teeth; then find (by trial) a centre from which to
strike a curve approximating to the hypocycloidal curve,
and commence to put in the faces of the teeth in pencil,
and afterwards in ink.

Secondly, divide the pitch circle of pinion into 22 equal
parts (the number of teeth), commencing from B, the
line of centres; and find the epicycloidal curve B k for
the faces of the teeth of pinion, by rolling (as described,
Art. 57) upon the pitch circle B E, the generating circle
N B L, whose diameter is equal to A B, the radius of the
wheel. Set off the thickness of teeth on the pitch circle
of pinion; and, having found a radius for the epicycloid,
proceed to put in the curves with a bow pen. The flanks
of the teeth are, in both cases, radial lines, and may be
drawn within $\frac{1}{15}$th of the pitch from the root, and joined
thereto by curves (Art. 53) for strengthening the teeth,
which is very desirable in this form of wheel.

TEETH OF SPUR WHEELS PRACTICALLY CONSIDERED.

Art. 97.—The mode of describing the teeth of an
annular wheel and pinion to work together has been ex-

G

plained in the preceding article. It may also be taken for
granted that the teeth of a pair of spur wheels will work
correctly if constructed in the same manner, that is, by
employing two generating circles whose diameters are
respectively equal to the radii of the two wheels intended to work together, the *larger* generating circle
being employed for obtaining the faces of the teeth of
pinion, and the *smaller* for obtaining the faces of the
teeth of *wheel;* the flanks in both cases being radial lines.
But the impossibility of making a third wheel of other
dimensions that will work correctly in the same train
must at once be acknowledged; inasmuch as another
generating circle is introduced to describe a curve which
has already been defined, namely, that of the wheel with
which it is to gear. This difficulty is got over by employing *the same generating circle* for the *flanks* as well as
the *faces* of the teeth of what is commonly called a set of
wheels of any given pitch.

ART. 98.—Now the question is, whether the flanks and
faces should be *arcs of circles* or epicycloids? Admitting,
on the authority of mathematicians, that the epicycloid
for the face and the hypocycloid for the flank are the best
for producing a constant velocity ratio, the only thing to
be settled is *the diameter of generating circle*, commonly
called the " scriber." The importance of some definite
system being adopted is manifested by the fact that *two
wheels of any given pitch from different makers will not
work together,* for the simple reason that each firm adopts
a rule or formula of its own for the shape of the teeth,
believing, no doubt, that it is the best.

This anomaly is illustrated by Drawing L, which
represents the forms of teeth at present made by four of
the most respectable firms in Lancashire and Yorkshire,
who have most kindly furnished the writer with particulars of their practice. The illustrations are of a wheel
29·92 inches diameter, with 47 teeth, 2 inch pitch—the
teeth being drawn full size, that the forms of the curves

may be clearly seen. The flanks and faces of the teeth in
No. 1 are arcs of circles whose radii = the pitch ; the
flank being struck from a centre n in the pitch circle, and
the face from a point m in a circle concentric with the
pitch line. The distance between the concentric circles
was not stated ; it appears, however, to be about $\frac{1}{13}$th of
the pitch, which will be near enough for our present
purpose.

The makers of No. 2 say, " In setting out the teeth of
wheels, we invariably strike the circle of tooth with a
radius of the pitch of wheel, making the thickness of the
point of tooth $\frac{4}{5}$ths of the thickness of tooth for wheels
where there is no very great difference between size of
wheel and pinion; but where the pinion is much smaller
than wheel, we reduce the thickness of the point of tooth
of pinion as may be required." It will be observed that
the flanks in this case are radial lines.

Without remarking on the merits or demerits of any
particular form of tooth, we shall proceed to the makers
of No. 3, who say, " We adopt the following method for
scribing circle for spur wheels :—

" Pitch × 2·5."

Now, this rule gives to the " scriber " a diameter which
is a fraction *less* than the radius of the least wheel of the
set, *to which* 16 *teeth are assigned*; the fraction being
·058 inch for 1¼ inch pitch, and ·278 inch for 6 inches
pitch. Thus, 1·25 × 2·5 = 3·125 for the diameter of
scriber, and

$$\frac{1·25 \times 16}{3·1416} = 6·366$$

$$6·366 \div 2 = 3·183$$

$$3·183 - 3·125 = ·058$$

of an inch less than the radius of a pinion with 16 teeth ;
it will therefore be sufficient for our purpose to take this
number as representing the least wheel of the set. By a
set of wheels is meant all sizes of wheels of a given pitch ;
therefore, to apply the rule in the present case, we have

G 2

2·5 × 2 = 5 inches for the diameter of generating circle for 2 inches pitch.

No. 4. The principle adopted by this firm is to "suppose the *least* diameter of any wheel that *can* be, or probably will be, required for any given pitch, *half of which* is the diameter of generating circle." They consequently make use of the following sizes:—

For 1 inch, 1¼ inch and 1½ inch pitch, 3 inches diameter
  „   1¾ „   2   „   „   2¼   „   5 „   „
  „   2½ „   2¾ „   „   3   „   9 „   „

The diameter of generatrix for 2 inches pitch being the same in the two last cases will account for No. 3 and No. 4 being identical; had the pitch selected been 3 inches, we should then have had four different forms of teeth, because 2·5 × 3 = 7·5, the diameter of scriber for No. 3, while the diameter for No. 4 would be 9 inches.

So far as our own practice extends, we have for many years past advocated and erected a number of wheels having the "Odontograph" form of tooth, which was invented by Professor Willis, and published in his "Principles of Mechanism" in 1841. We have preferred it on these grounds, viz., that the form of tooth is strong, works accurately with very little clearance, and is based on mathematical principles. For some cause or other, this ingeniously contrived instrument has not found much favour with the pattern-maker, who probably finds it easier to "strike" out a tooth with the "scriber," which he understands, than with the "Odontograph," which we will now explain as nearly as possible in the learned Professor's own words.

THE ODONTOGRAPH.

ART. 99.—Figure 26 on the opposite page represents the instrument about half the size of the original; and, as it is merely formed out of a sheet of card-board, this

Fig. 26.

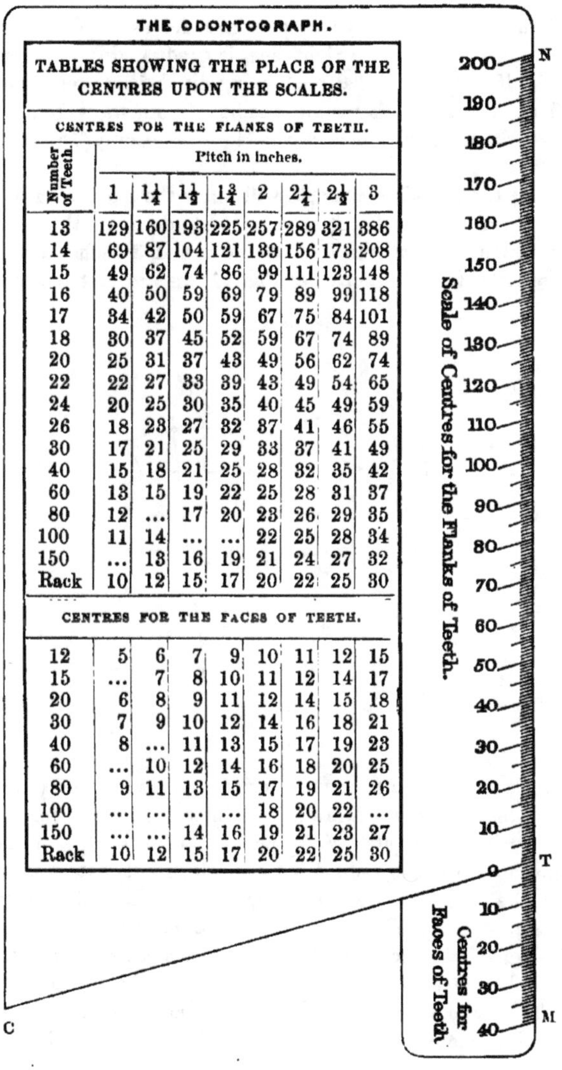

THE ODONTOGRAPH.

TABLES SHOWING THE PLACE OF THE CENTRES UPON THE SCALES.

CENTRES FOR THE FLANKS OF TEETH.

Number of Teeth	Pitch in inches.							
	1	1¼	1½	1¾	2	2¼	2½	3
13	129	160	193	225	257	289	321	386
14	69	87	104	121	139	156	173	208
15	49	62	74	86	99	111	123	148
16	40	50	59	69	79	89	99	118
17	34	42	50	59	67	75	84	101
18	30	37	45	52	59	67	74	89
20	25	31	37	43	49	56	62	74
22	22	27	33	39	43	49	54	65
24	20	25	30	35	40	45	49	59
26	18	23	27	32	37	41	46	55
30	17	21	25	29	33	37	41	49
40	15	18	21	25	28	32	35	42
60	13	15	19	22	25	28	31	37
80	12	...	17	20	23	26	29	35
100	11	14	...	...	22	25	28	34
150	...	13	16	19	21	24	27	32
Rack	10	12	15	17	20	22	25	30

CENTRES FOR THE FACES OF TEETH.

	1	1¼	1½	1¾	2	2¼	2½	3
12	5	6	7	9	10	11	12	15
15	...	7	8	10	11	12	14	17
20	6	8	9	11	12	14	15	18
30	7	9	10	12	14	16	18	21
40	8	...	11	13	15	17	19	23
60	...	10	12	14	16	18	20	25
80	9	11	13	15	17	19	21	26
100	...	...	...	...	18	20	22	...
150	...	...	14	16	19	21	23	27
Rack	10	12	15	17	20	22	25	30

N

200
190
180
170
160
150
140
130
120
110
100
90
80
70
60
50
40
30
20
10

Scale of Centres for the Flanks of Teeth.

T

10
20
30
40

Centres for Faces of Teeth.

C

M

figure will enable any one to make it for use. The edge,
N T M, which forms a right line, is graduated into a scale
of half inches, each half inch being divided into ten parts.
The half inch divisions are numbered both ways from T;
and the edge T C makes an angle of exactly 75° with
N T M.

ART. 100.—One example will show the mode of using
this instrument. Let it be required to delineate the form
of a tooth for a wheel of 29 teeth and 3 inches pitch.
Describe from a centre A, Fig. 27, an arc of the given

Fig. 27.

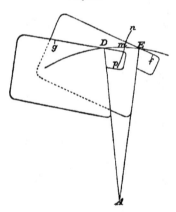

pitch circle; and upon it set off D E, equal to the pitch,
and bisect it in *m*. Draw radial lines D A, E A. For the
arc within the pitch circle apply the slant edge of the
instrument to the radial line A D, placing its extremity D
on the pitch circle, as in the figure. In the table headed
Centres for the Flanks of Teeth, look down the column of
3-inch pitch, and opposite 30 teeth, which is the nearest
number to that required, will be found the number 49.
The point *g,* indicated on the drawing board by the position
of this number on the scale of equal parts, marked *Scale*

of Centres for the Flanks of Teeth, is the centre required, from which the arc *m p* must be drawn with the radius *g m.*

The centre for the arc *m n*, or face, which lies outside the pitch circle, is found, in like manner, by applying the slant edge of the instrument to the radial line E A. The number 21 obtained from the lower table will indicate the position *f* of the required centre upon the lower scale. In using the instrument it is only necessary to recollect that the scale employed and the point *m* always lie on the two opposite sides of the radial line to which the instrument is applied.

The curve *n m p* is also true for an annular wheel of the same radius and number of teeth, *n* becoming the root and *p* the point of the teeth. For a rack, the pitch line D E becomes a right line, and D A, E A, perpendiculars to it, at a distance equal to the pitch.

Numbers for pitches not inserted in the tables may be obtained by direct proportion from the column of some other pitch; thus, for 4-inch pitch by doubling those of 2-inch, and for $\frac{1}{2}$-inch pitch by halving those of 1-inch pitch. Also, no tabular numbers are given for twelve teeth in the upper table, because within the pitch circle their teeth are radial lines. *Prof. Willis' Mechanism, Arts.* 142 *and* 143.

ART. 101.—Now, the same form and proportions of tooth as obtained by the odontograph can be produced by rolling a generating circle of given diameter upon the pitch line in the usual manner, with the advantage (if any can be claimed for so short a curve) of substituting the epicycloid and hypocycloid for arcs of circles. In practice, we find the diameter of generating circle for 1-inch pitch to be 1·59 inch, and for 2 inches pitch 3·18 inches, and that these diameters are respectively equal to the radii of wheels with ten teeth. Again, for 3 inches pitch, we find the diameter of scriber to be 5·729 inches, which is equal to the radius of a pinion with *twelve teeth*, and that these scribers produce the odontograph form of tooth, which we have advocated for years, and, with slight modifications, shall continue to do so.

ART. 102.—Having explained *five* different rules or methods of striking out the teeth of wheels, to which five others might be added, and knowing from experience that a preference is given to the use of the scriber on account of the facility of obtaining the most correct form of tooth, we venture to suggest, for the consideration of engineers, especially those who are engaged in mill work, the propriety of adopting a system that will be universal, and so get rid of these anomalous and unsatisfactory rules, without material change of that form of tooth which is generally admitted to be the strongest and best adapted for producing equable motion. The system for mill-gearing which the author is about to propose and illustrate is as follows:—

1. *That there shall be a generating circle for every pitch, and that the pitch be stamped or otherwise marked on each "scriber" or generating circle.*

2. *That the diameter of each generating circle be equal to the radius of the least wheel of the set.*

3. *That the number of teeth assigned to the least wheel be* 14 *for all sets of wheels for mill gearing.*

The adoption of such a system, whatever may be the number of teeth assigned to the least wheel, would ensure perfect regularity and uniformity with all makers, and we see no reason why this should not be the case in the manufacture of gearing as well as gauges, &c.*

If we assume *fourteen* as the number of teeth for the smallest wheel in each set, the formula for scribers will be

$$\frac{P \times 7}{3\cdot1416} = d,$$ in which P is the pitch and d the diameter of scriber for any given set. The diameters of scribers for

---

* We allude to the admirable system of gauges introduced by Mr. Whitworth.

pitches from 1 inch up to $3\frac{1}{2}$ inches, advancing by $\frac{1}{4}$ inch, will therefore be as follow :—

TABLE OF GENERATING CIRCLES FOR THE TEETH OF WHEELS.

Pitch in Inches.	1	1¼	1½	1¾	2	2¼	2½	2¾	3	3¼	3½
Diameter of Generator or Scriber.	2·228	2·785	3·342	3·899	4·456	5·013	5·57	6·127	6·684	7·241	7·798

In order that the form of tooth thus obtained may be judged of and compared with other forms, we must refer the reader to No. 1, Drawing M, which represents portions of two geared wheels of 30 and 60 teeth, 1-inch pitch, the action of the pair being directly on the line of centres, and to No. 2, which shows portions of two wheels of 44 and 47 teeth, 2 inches pitch, the action being some little distance from the line of centres ; but in either case it will he found to commence and leave off at about half the pitch from the line A B C ; therefore, the strength of a single tooth (hereafter to be noticed) will, other things being equal, represent the strength of the wheel.

It was formerly the practice to make the teeth of such a shape that two or more pairs would be in action at the same time; thus, by increasing the size of generating circle, the teeth of No. 2, Drawing M, could be made to fulfil these conditions; the effect, however, would be to diminish the thickness of the teeth at the base, and so reduce their strength; also, to increase the friction, by increasing the sliding action of the faces of those teeth adjoining the line of centres against the flanks of the teeth with which they are in contact. Moreover, this system is a departure from the first principle of *rolling contact*, and introduces a confusion of scribers, made according to taste, or to meet particular cases, which for ordinary mill-gearing we deem unnecessary, as all the wheels of a set will work accurately together if the flanks and faces of the teeth *are struck with the same describing circle.*

As a further comparison of the form of tooth here proposed, we will once more refer the reader to No. 5, Drawing L, which will be found to approximate to the forms shown at No. 3 and No. 4; the only difference being that they are a trifle larger at the base of tooth and a little more pointed, *but not so much as the odontograph*, the form of which is represented by the dotted line, *c d e*, No. 5. This difference is accounted for by the least wheel of the set belonging to Nos. 3 and 4 having 16 teeth, and that of the odontograph from 10 to 12; whereas the number which the author submits for consideration is 14.

We believe that a system called the *universal epicycloidal system* has before been proposed, but, so far as we can understand, not definitely, inasmuch as the diameter of scriber was left to the judgment of each maker.

The student will understand the use of the " scriber " from the following description.

GENERATING CIRCLE OR SCRIBER.

ART. 103.—A and A′, in the accompanying Fig. 28, represent a front and edge view of a generating circle or scriber for a set of wheels of a given pitch. It is made of a piece of pine, or other suitable material, about $\frac{1}{8}$ of an inch thick. On the face of A is screwed, and capable of adjustment, a projecting arm *b*, with a steel point *c* for marking out the curves. B B is a segment of wood, whose convex and concave edges are described with the same radius as the pitch circle of the wheel required to be constructed. C is a thin slip of wood, whose upper edge is of the same radius as the points of the teeth, and lower edge the same as the inside of the rim of wheel, with the pitch line *n* marked thereon. A number of points representing the thickness and spaces of the teeth must now be accurately set off on the pitch line *n*, and the thin slip secured with a couple of sprigs to the segment B, so that the line *n* coincides with the upper edge of B, as shown

at c^1, when the apparatus will be ready for describing the
faces of the teeth.   If A and the segment B were now
brought together, the slip c^1 would pass between the arm
b and wood circle (see edge view A′).   Therefore, by

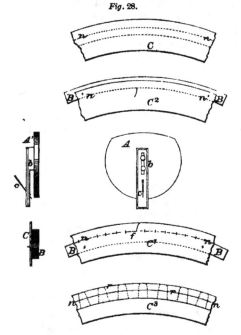

Fig. 28.

rolling the circle on the convex edge of B, the steel point
will describe an epicycloid, and thus mark on the slip c^1
the curve f, which is one face of a tooth; by rolling the
circle in the opposite direction the other face will be
described; and so on for any number of teeth.   In order
to describe the flanks, the pitch line n is made to coincide
with the concave edge of B, as shown at c^2; and the slip
is once more secured to the segment B.   If the generating
circle A be now inverted and the parts once more brought

together, the flanks or hypocycloidal curves may be
described by rolling the circle on the concave edge of B,
which, it will be remembered, is of the same curvature as
the pitch circle of the wheel.

ART. 104.—A number of teeth having been thus described on the slip, as shown at c^3, a templet of six or
more accurately formed teeth is obtained by carefully
removing the parts r r which form the spaces.   This
templet is applied to the rim or face of the "blank"
wheel or pattern, and the teeth marked out with a sharp
point; the templet is then shifted, and another series of
teeth marked out; and so on for the entire number.   It
will therefore be seen that all compass-work on the face
of the pattern is entirely avoided, and much time is
consequently saved by reducing the tedious work of
dividing a large circle into a given number of equal parts
to the simple operation of producing some half dozen
accurately formed teeth.

ART. 105.—Having alluded to the blank wheel or pattern
(a most expensive structure, which will be found fully
described in the "Practical Draughtsman's Book of Industrial Design" by Mr. Johnson,), we may observe that
such structures are rapidly being dispensed with.   All
that is now necessary to form the matrix is a pattern of
two or more teeth and a portion of the rim, which is
placed in a machine so arranged as to carry the model
teeth about a circle coinciding with the pitch circle; and
in this manner the teeth of wheels are moulded two or more
at a time.   This entire revolution in wheel pattern making,
as our friend the Mayor of Oldham (Mr. William Rye)
terms it, will effect an immense saving in the expense of
engineers' patterns, and also in room for stowage.   In
place of 14 or 16 days required to build up a pattern and
cast a wheel on the old system, as many hours only
are now necessary; in ordinary cases the pattern can
be made and the casting delivered the day following
the order.

BACK LASH.

ART. 106.—In wheels that have a greater amount of clearance between the teeth than is necessary, when the motion of the driver is retarded the acting surfaces of the teeth will be withdrawn, and on the motion of the driver being accelerated the flanks and faces of the teeth will strike violently against each other. To obviate this back lash, we recommend less clearance between the teeth than that usually allowed.

Some years since the writer erected a pair of engines with a fly spur wheel 18 feet $4\frac{1}{2}$ inches, and pinion 9 feet $3\frac{1}{4}$ inches, iron and iron, in which the clearance was only $\frac{1}{20}$th of an inch, or $\frac{1}{60}$th of the pitch; the form of tooth being the "odontograph." These wheels worked with admirable precision for several years, when a mortise pinion was introduced to lessen the noise in the engine-house. For the present form of gearing this amount will be considered too little; but with teeth properly formed, and moulded with that accuracy which is attainable by a moulding machine, we should consider $\frac{1}{20}$th of an inch for 3 inches pitch sufficient and effectual in removing the evil effects of back lash. All that is necessary with properly formed teeth is an amount of clearance that will prevent rubbing, and allow for any inequality in the casting.

FORMULA FOR THE STRENGTH OF TEETH OF WHEELS.

ART. 107.—M. Morin, in his "Aide Mémoire Mécanique Pratique," gives it as a rule that when the velocity of the pitch circle does not exceed 5 feet per second, the *breadth* of the tooth ought to be equal to 4 times the thickness; but when the velocity is higher, the breadth ought to be equal to 5 times the thickness. If the teeth be constantly wet, as in the case of water-wheels, he recommends 6 times the thickness at all velocities. The usual practice of our engineers is $2\frac{1}{4}$ times the pitch, or 5 times the thickness of tooth.

With regard to the thickness of the tooth, it is manifest that it must be dependent on the pressure required to be sustained. This relation may be conveniently expressed for all cases by the formula

$$t = c \sqrt{P},$$

where t is the thickness of tooth, P the pressure upon it in lbs., and c a constant multiplier depending upon the nature of the material of which the tooth is formed.

To find the value of c, put a to represent the known strength of a bar 1 inch long, 1 inch thick, and 1 inch broad; then to support a weight w by a bar of a length l and breadth b, the thickness t must, according to the received formula for the strength of material, be in the relation

$$t = \sqrt{\frac{P \times l}{a \times b}}.$$

Now, on the assumption that a portion only of the breadth of the tooth equal to twice the length ought to be taken into the calculation, because a tooth is liable to fracture across the corner (and this hypothesis is a perfectly safe one), we have $b = 2 \cdot l$; whence

$$t = \sqrt{\frac{P \times l}{a \times b}} = \sqrt{\frac{P \times l}{a \times 2l}} = \sqrt{\frac{P}{2a}}.$$

Taking $a = 8,000$ lbs. for cast iron, we have $2a = 16,000$ lbs., estimated as dead weight, which is about ten times greater than the working pressure that such a bar ought to be made to sustain; consequently the practical value of $2a$ may be taken at 1,600 lbs.; and accordingly

$$t = \sqrt{\frac{P}{2a}} = \sqrt{\frac{P}{1600}} = \tfrac{1}{40}\sqrt{P} = \cdot025\sqrt{P}.$$

Therefore, for cast iron $c = \cdot025$; in the same way we get for brass, $c = \cdot035$, and for hardwood, $c = \cdot038$; consequently, for the thickness of teeth of these materials, we have

$$t = \cdot025 \sqrt{\text{p}} \text{ for cast iron,}$$
$$t = \cdot035 \sqrt{\text{p}} \text{ for brass,}$$
$$t = \cdot038 \sqrt{\text{p}} \text{ for hardwood,}$$

p being the pressure on the tooth in lbs., and t the thickness of tooth in inches and parts of an inch.

Example.—Let it be required to find the thickness of a tooth which is to sustain a pressure of 3,510 lbs., the material being cast iron; in this case

$$\text{p} = 3510; \text{ therefore } \sqrt{\text{p}} = 59\cdot25$$
$$\text{and } t = \cdot025 \sqrt{\text{p}} = \cdot025 \times 59\cdot25 = 1\cdot48 \text{ inch.}$$

We have found the above formula to agree in a most remarkable manner with the best practice, yet should be inclined to make the tooth a little stronger if the breadth of tooth were only twice the length; but for wheels of ordinary breadth ($2\frac{1}{2}$ times the pitch) we think it may be relied upon.

To find the Number of Horses' Power* that a Wheel is capable of transmitting at any given velocity.

ART. 108.—The principal difficulty that presents itself to the tyro is to select, from the many rules for solving questions of this kind, one that he can rely on in practice. To enter into an elaborate explanation of all these rules would not only be inconsistent with the object of this work, but greatly in the way of the student's progress towards a solution of such a question as the following :

Let it be required to determine the strength, in horses' power, of a wheel 6 inches pitch and 16 inches broad, when moving with a velocity of 16 feet per second; the thickness of tooth being 2·94 inches and length 4 inches.

* A horse power is equal to what is now commonly called 33,000 " foot pounds:" that is, 33,000 lbs. raised one foot high in one minute.

ART. 109.—The two rules which are most prominently before us are known as Roberton's and Carmichael's; and in order more fully to explain our reasons for adopting one of these rules in preference to the other, we have selected an extreme case, but still a case in practice to which all rules that deserve that name ought to apply.

Mr. Roberton's rule is this :—The strength of the teeth is ascertained by multiplying the square of their thickness by their breadth, taken in inches and parts of an inch; and the number that represents the strength will indicate the number of horses' power, at a velocity of about 4 feet per second: that is, $t^2 \times b =$ the number of horses' power that the wheel is capable of transmitting when moving with a velocity of 4 feet per second.

We would observe, with regard to this rule, that the *length* of the tooth as an element in all calculations is entirely omitted; and if we may be allowed to look upon the tooth of a wheel in the light of a cantilever, the strength of which it is impossible to calculate without the *length*, we cannot but think the omission of importance. For instance, let Fig. 29 represent a cantilever 1 inch long, 1 inch thick, and 1 inch deep; and let the breaking weight

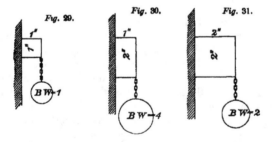

Fig. 29.   *Fig. 30.*   *Fig. 31.*

be *one*, say one ton. Now, if we make the depth of the cantilever 2 inches, as shown at Fig. 30, the breaking weight will be 4 tons, being as the square of the depth. But if at the same time we double the length, as exhibited at Fig. 31, the breaking weight will be 2 tons; that is inversely as the *length* and as the square of the depth.

Now each of these figures may be looked upon as a tooth of a wheel, the strength of which is inversely as the length.

ART. 110.—Mr. Carmichael's rule, which we have used for many years, is this :—*Multiply the breadth of the teeth by the square of the thickness, and divide the product by the length; the quotient will be the proportional strength in horses' power, with a velocity of 2·27 feet per second.*

The above being the elements for estimating the breaking weight of a lever fixed at one end and loaded at the other, we will now see how the two rules agree with the wheel in question (ART. 108), which is a fraction over 19 feet 1 inch diameter, with 120 teeth, pitch 6 inches, thickness of tooth 2·94 inches, length of tooth 4 inches, breadth 16 inches, and thickness of rim $4\frac{5}{8}$ inches. This wheel, which the writer has seen at work, is keyed on the crank shaft of an engine of the following dimensions:—

Diameter of cylinder 45 inches = 1,590·4 inches area.
Length of stroke . . . 8 feet.
Number of strokes . . . 16.
Effective pressure of steam . = 20 lbs.

The power of this engine will therefore be—

$$\frac{1,590{\cdot}4 \times 20 \times (8 \times 2 \times 16)}{33,000} = 246{\cdot}75 \text{ horses;}$$

and adopting Mr. Carmichael's formula for the strength of the wheel we have—

$$\frac{t^2\, b}{l} = \frac{2{\cdot}94^2 \times 16}{4} = 34{\cdot}57 \text{ horses' power}$$

at 2·27 feet per second.

Now the circumference of the wheel being 60 feet, the velocity at the pitch circle will be exactly 16 feet per second. Hence we have

$$\frac{34{\cdot}57 \times 16}{2{\cdot}27} = 243{\cdot}66 \text{ horses' power,}$$

the actual power of engine being 246·75 horses.

H

ART. 111.—Again, we have 1,590 square inches (area of piston) × 20 lbs. = 31,800 lbs. pressure on the piston. The length of crank = 4 feet, and radius of driving wheel = 9·5 feet; consequently $\dfrac{31,800 \times 4}{9\cdot5} = 13,389$ lbs. acting at the pitch line.

Now the thickness of tooth, according to ART. 107, will be ·025 $\sqrt{}$ 13,389 = ·025 × 115·7 = 2·89 inches, the actual thickness in practice being 2·94 inches, showing a difference of ·05 = $\frac{5}{100} = \frac{1}{20}$th of an inch.

It may be worthy of note that the fracture of one of the segments of this wheel, when driving two rail mills, each with two pairs of rolls, and five pairs of other rolls, in all nine pairs of rolls, rendered it necessary to increase the breadth 2 inches and thickness of rim 1 inch, making the wheel 18 inches on the face, with a rim $5\frac{4}{8}$ inches thick.

ART. 112.—Although the two rules known as Roberton's and Carmichael's will, in many cases, be found to agree pretty nearly up to 3 inches pitch, there is a wide difference in the case before us. We have shown the power of engine to be = 246·75 horses; and the strength of wheel, by Mr. Carmichael's rule, = 243·66 horses. But, with Mr. Roberton's rule, we get $t^2\,b = 2\cdot94^2 \times 16 = 138\cdot3$ at 4 feet per second. The power at any other velocity being found by proportion, we have 4 : 16 :: 138·3 : 553·2, the horses' power at 16 feet per second; or, 307 horses in excess of the load by which the wheel was fractured. We therefore recommend the following rule :—

$$\frac{t^2\,b}{l} = \text{H.P. at } 2\cdot27 \text{ feet per second;}$$

and, for the thickness of tooth—

$\sqrt{}$ P × ·025 = t for cast iron
$\sqrt{}$ P × ·035 = t „ brass
$\sqrt{}$ P × ·038 = t „ hardwood

in which P = the stress in lbs.

PROBLEM XV.

The effective pressure on the piston of an engine is 13,017 *lbs., the length of crank* 2 *feet* 3 *inches, and the radius of driving wheel* 41·1 *inches, what ought to be the thickness of the teeth of wheel when of cast iron?*

ART. 113.—The answer is 2·3 inches. The actual thickness, as we found it in practice, was 2·15 inches; the difference 0·15 being in favour of the rule.

PROBLEM XVI.

The velocity of piston in the above case was 225 *feet per minute, diameter of cylinder* 25¼ *inches, effective pressure* 25 *lbs., it is required to find the horses' power of the engine, and also that of the wheel, which made* 25 *revolutions per minute; thickness of tooth being* 2·3 *inches, length* 3·2 *inches, and breadth* 12 *inches.*

ART. 114.—*Answer.*—The power of engine = 89 horses; and the power of wheel = 78·2 horses. The above particulars are from the writer's notes on indicator diagrams, taken in 1851. The wheel in question is still at work.

CHAPTER X.

Spur, Bevel, Skew, and other Gearing.

It frequently happens in the construction of plans and elevations of machinery that the axis of a wheel or pulley may be parallel to the horizontal plane, but inclined to the vertical plane, and *vice versâ*. In either case the projection of a wheel in such a position as that shown at No. 1, Drawing N, becomes a matter of necessity; hence we have the following problem.

Problem XVII.

Required the projection of a spur wheel, in a plane which makes an angle of 37° with the vertical plane and 90° with the horizontal plane.

Art. 115.—Fig. 32. Draw ɪ ʟ, the intersecting line of the two planes of projection. From any point *a* draw *a b*, making the required angle of 37° with ɪ ʟ; and from any convenient point *c*, in *a b*, draw the perpendicular *c d* of indefinite length. Take any point *e*, in *c d*, as a centre, and describe a semi-circle of the same radius as the wheel at the point of tooth; and through *e* draw *f g*, parallel to *a b*. If lines be now drawn from *f* and *g*, perpendicular to *a b*, and a line *f′ g′* parallel to *g f*, or *a b*, making *h f′*, or *b g′*, equal to the breadth of the wheel, the horizontal projection, No. 1, of the wheel at the required angle will be obtained.

Again, if from any point c a semicircle be drawn with the same radius *e f* or *e g*, the major and minor axes of the ellipses in No. 2 will be obtained by drawing vertical lines from *g′ i′ f′*, No. 1, to intersect horizontal lines drawn from *i q p*, as shown by construction. Find the projection of ellipses (as directed by Art. 122, Elem. Treat.) for the *point*, *pitch line*, and *root* of tooth; and, having completed the geometrical projection of teeth in No. 1, as *p n m o*, proceed to find their projection on

Fig. 32.

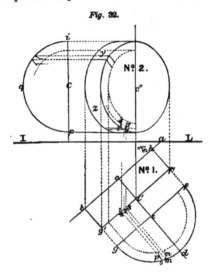

No. 2, by drawing lines from *p n m o*, parallel to *c d*, cutting line *g' f'*, in 1, 2, 3, 4; and from these points draw lines perpendicular to I L, to cut the ellipses representing the pitch line and point of tooth in points 1', 2', 3', 4'.

NOTE.—The intersections of the ellipses being difficult to determine as the vertical lines 1 1', 2 2', approach *g'* and *f'*, the projections of the teeth from *y* to *z*, on each side of the wheel, should be obtained from the geometrical projection *i q p*. Four points are required for the projection of each tooth, when the faces may be drawn in with the aid of a small French curve. The flanks, being radial lines, must be drawn to converge in the projected centre *c''* of the wheel No. 2. Points for the projection of the arms are obtained in like manner from the two geometrical projections. It is only necessary to remark that an even number of teeth in the wheel, as shown in the complete wheel (No. 1, Drawing N), will give the student much less trouble than an uneven number.

BEVEL WHEELS.

ART. 116.—When rotary motion is to be given to two shafts that lie in the same plane, but in an angular direction to each other, the wheels employed are called bevel or conical wheels, from their being constructed in the form of a pair of cones, the apices of which *will always be found in the point of intersection of the centre lines of the two shafts;* the bases of the cones being to each other as the number of teeth in one wheel is to the number of teeth in the other wheel, or as the velocity of the driver is to the velocity of the follower.

PROBLEM XVIII.

Required the form of the cones for a pair of bevel wheels, when the two shafts are at right angles to each other, and the velocity ratio equal.

Fig. 33.

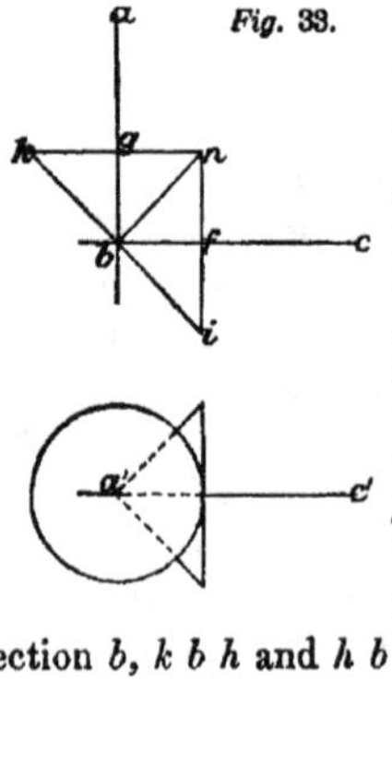

ART. 117.—Fig. 33. Let $a\,b$, $b\,c$, be the two shafts, at right angles to each other. From b, along $b\,c$, set off the radius of driver = 1, in point f; and from b, along $b\,a$, set off the radius of follower = 1, in point g. Through f and g draw lines perpendicular to the two axes $a\,b$, $b\,c$, meeting in h; make $f\,i$ equal to $f\,h$, and $g\,k$ equal to $g\,h$. If lines be now drawn from k, h, i, to the point of intersection b, $k\,b\,h$ and $h\,b\,i$ will represent the required form

of cones for what would be called a pair of "mitre wheels," the axes being in the same plane. See a' c', which is a plan of the two cones. The term mitre is only applied when the bases of the cones k h and h i are equal, and the axes at right angles; in all other cases the term " bevel " is used.

PROBLEM XIX.

Required the frustums of two cones for a pair of bevel wheels, the shafts being at right angles and the velocity ratio as 2 to 1.

ART. 118.—Let a b, b c, Fig. 34, represent the axes of the shafts; and let a b, the follower, make twice the number of revolutions in the same time as b c, the driver.

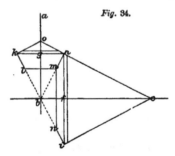

Fig. 34.

Make b f equal to the radius of small cone $= 1$, and through f draw a line perpendicular to b c. Make b g equal to twice b $f = 2$; then through g draw the perpendicular h k; and make g $k = g$ h, and f $i = f$ h. If lines be now drawn from i h k to meet in b, the point of intersection, k b h and i b h will represent the form of cones for a pair of bevel wheels as required.

Again, make k l equal to the breadth of wheel on the

face; draw *l m* parallel to *k h*, cutting *h b* in *m*; and from *m* draw *m n* parallel to *h i*: then will *k l m h*, *h m n i*, be the frustums required, and *k h*, *i h* the pitch lines of the two wheels.

The form of a bevel wheel, however, is that of a double cone, or two frustums joined at their bases. The apices of the second pair of frustums is found by drawing through *h*, Fig. 34, a line *perpendicular* to *h b*, intersecting the two lines of shafts in *c* and *o*, which will be the apices of the cones *k o h* and *h c i*: therefore, lines drawn parallel to *k h*, *h i*, will give the frustum, or that part of a bevel wheel on which the length of the teeth is shown, as will hereafter be explained.

To avoid a very common mistake, the *perpendicular* to *h b* should be remembered; it is the same in all cases, whatever may be the angle of the axes or radii of the wheels, as shown in Fig. 35, to which the foregoing description and letters of reference will apply.

Fig. 35.

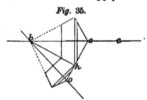

When designing machinery, bevel wheels are represented as above; but in finished drawings the projections of the teeth are indispensable.

TEETH OF BEVEL WHEELS.

ART. 119.—*Example* 1. Let *h h'*, No. 4, Drawing N, represent the pitch line and also the diameter of a mitre wheel. Find the apex of each cone, as directed (Art. 118); produce *c h* indefinitely; and make $h\,t = \frac{5}{18}$ths and $h\,s = \frac{6}{18}$ths of the pitch: then will *s t* represent the length of the tooth. From *t* and *s*, the point and root, draw lines parallel to *h h'*, cutting *c t'* in *t'*, *s'*; and from *t*, *s*, and *t'*, *s'* draw lines meeting in point *b*. Make *t l* equal to breadth of wheel on the face; and draw *l m parallel* to *t c*: then will *t l n s* represent a side elevation of a tooth, and *m* the radiating centre for the teeth inside the wheel;—*s n p* being a section of the rim.

To obtain projection No. 3, describe four concentric circles, respectively of the same radius as the radius of the wheel at the points *t*, *l*, and roots *n*, *s*, as shown by horizontal dotted lines drawn from those points. Having divided the great circle, represented by *t t'*, for the teeth of the wheel, draw lines converging to the common centre of the concentric circles (*m'*, No. 3), and they will represent the direction of the faces of each tooth; the teeth are distinguished by leaving out portions of the circles at *r, r*, as will be understood.

Again, the projection of the teeth in No. 2, which represents an edge view of No. 3, is shown by the construction lines for one tooth. The two points *z* are obtained by drawing lines from *y* parallel to the axis *o' b'*, and so on for each tooth; the root of tooth is found by the intersection of lines drawn from *z* to *o'* as shown, and the face, or flank and face, by drawing lines from the point and root to converge in *b'*, &c.

ART. 120.—*Example* 2. Nos. 5 and 6, Drawing N. The teeth in this case having curved faces and radial flanks, it will be necessary to find the projection of four points for each tooth, as shown by construction lines *x x'*, No. 5. These points being joined by curved lines to represent the faces of the teeth, the flanks will be drawn to converge in *c''*, and for the inside of the wheel in *m''*. See, also, the section of the bevel wheel, in which the lines converge in c^3 m^3.

In delineating the teeth of spur wheels (Art. 53) we take the centre of one tooth and outer side of the next adjoining as a radius for the curved faces. In bevel wheels,

however, we take the centre of a space, as at A, No. 5,
and outer side of the tooth adjoining as a radius for the
curved face; the radius being increased in the same ratio
as the angle which the shafts make with each other is
diminished, or, as the form of bevel approaches that of a
spur wheel. The curved face (shown at x', which is a
back elevation of the pinion, and at t' in No. 6, which is
a front elevation of the wheel) is not obtained by any
rule, although the absolute form of curve can, if required,
be found by projection, and a consideration of the development of conical surfaces as explained in Elem. Treat.,
Arts. 159 to 163. From these Articles it will be manifest
that C D, C F (No. 5), described from c'', c^3 as centres,
will be the envelopes of the two frustums; that the geometrical projection of the required form of tooth upon such
envelopes would if applied to the frustums give the
required form of tooth for each bevel; and that such
teeth if projected on the surfaces (frustums) of the two
cones, will work with the same amount of accuracy as
C D, C F would upon the surface of two cylinders with
c'' c^3 for the line of centres.

ART. 121.—*Example* 3. Drawing O represents a frame-
work *s s*, supporting four circularly grooved rollers 1, 2, 3, 4,
which were originally intended to compress and thereby
consolidate the plastic material of earthenware pipes by
forcing them over the end of a stationary mandrel A. The
rolls were driven by a pinion and spur wheel B; the latter
being keyed on the end of the shaft C, which gave motion
to the three pairs of mitre wheels D, D, D. These wheels
are introduced to the student merely as an example for
practice in the projection of mitre wheels with square
pointed teeth.

CROWN WHEELS.

ART. 122.—A modification of this form of wheel is
given at No. 1, Drawing P, of which we may observe that

anything like perfect action can seldom be attained on account of the unequal contraction of the casting, which pulls the rim of the wheel into all manner of shapes : the consequence is that in wheels of 4 feet 6 inches diameter and upwards a separation of the pitch circles to a considerable extent takes place several times in the course of a revolution.   To cast the rim in a separate piece with a provision for bolting to the arms would in all probability remedy the defect, but it would add considerably to the cost.   The above wheel is really a " bevel," although the term " crown " is sometimes applied.

ART. 123.—The teeth of a crown wheel proper are formed on the edge of a broad hoop, and they are consequently parallel to the axis, which may either be concentric with, or eccentric to, the hoop, as may be required for a constant or variable motion of the axis of the follower, which is at right angles to the driver.   The term crown wheel is also applied to a form of escapement called the " crown wheel escapement," used in common watches and clocks of the oldest date.

ARMS OF BEVEL WHEELS.

ART. 124.—The average dimensions for the rim and arms of a bevel wheel may be thus stated—see No. 2, Drawing P, which is a front elevation and section of a portion of a bevel wheel—

Make the thickness of rim through the centre $a\,b$ equal to half the pitch.

Make the thickness (breadth*) of face arm A and cross arm B equal to the thickness of rim at c.

----

* The terms breadth and depth have been employed in the illustration of spur wheels in the same sense as for the strength of materials; a beam, for instance, has length, breadth, and depth—breadth being synonymous with thickness, and depth with breadth : thus the breadth of a plank put edgewise will be the depth of the beam, &c.

Make the breadth (depth) of arm at the boss *e e* equal to ⅘ths the breadth of the face of wheel = *f g*, and reduce ¼ inch for every foot in length as it approaches the rim.

Make the length of boss *h i* ½ inch more than the breadth of wheel *f l*; and thickness of boss N equal to the pitch.

B′ A′ is a transverse section of the face and cross arm, taken through the line *r s*.

SKEW BEVELS.

ART. 125.—This is a form of gear designed to meet a particular case in roving and slubbing frames, where a number of vertical spindles are simultaneously driven by an axis which is at right angles to, *but not in the same plane*, as the axes of the followers; a condition that requires the teeth of each pair of wheels to be projected in a plane which is determined by the ratio of the two wheels that are to work together.

PROBLEM XX.

Required the inclination of the teeth to the axes of a pair of skew bevels, whose diameters at the pitch circles are 3 inches and 2 inches; the distance between the planes of the axes being ½ an inch; number of teeth in wheel 30 and in pinion 20. Drawing, full size.

ART. 126.—Let A and B, No. 3, Drawing P, represent an elevation of the axes; A being the driving shaft, and B one of the spindles of a fly frame for cotton spinning. From A and B let fall vertical lines A *a*, B *h* indefinitely; from any point *b*, draw *b a* perpendicular to B *h*; and divide *b a* in *c*, so that *a c* is to *b c* as the radius of the driver is to the radius of the follower. From *a* as a centre, and with *a d* the radius of driver, describe the pitch circle $d\ e$ (3 inches diameter); and from the same centre, with radius $a\ c$, describe the circle $c\ g$.   Again, from any convenient point b', and with the radius $b\ c$, describe the circle $b'\ c'$, also the pitch circle $h\ f$ of follower (2 inches diameter).

If a line be now drawn from c to c', such line will be tangential to the circles $c\ g$, $b'\ c'$, and give the inclination of the faces of the teeth to the axes of the pair of wheels: that is to say, all the faces of the teeth of wheel are drawn tangentially to the small circle $c\ g$; and the teeth of pinion tangentially to circle $b'\ c'$.   Imagine the pinion $h\ f$ to be turned upon $n\ m$, so that the axes of the pair are at right angles, then will the tooth f coincide with and be opposite the space e.

The direction of the teeth having been thus found, and the pitch circles divided (ART. 62) into the required number of equal parts, the faces of each tooth will be represented by two slightly dissimilar curves, caused by the angularity of the teeth, which in other respects may be described as directed for ordinary bevel wheels.

Wheels of this kind are only calculated for light work, on account of the amount of sliding action, which increases with the distance of the two axes.

NOTE.—The ratio of the small circles, $c\ g$, $b\ c$, to the radii of the wheels may be found geometrically;—thus, let $a\ b$, Fig. 4, ART. 54, represent the radii of the two wheels, and $g\ h$ the distance between the two axes; if a line be now drawn from a point in $a\ b$ to any point, as e, $g\ h$ will be divided in the same ratio as $a\ b$, and so give the radii of the small circles $c\ g$ and $b\ c$.

HELICAL WHEELS.

ART. 127.—Another form of wheel for the same purpose as the skew bevel is that shown at No. 4, Drawing P, which represents a pair of helical wheels, or as they are commonly (but erroneously) called *spiral* pinions or wheels. The teeth of these wheels, being at an angle of 45° to the axis, fit into and drive each other by a sliding but remarkably smooth action, that is in effect something like a good fitting nut and screw, which is really the character of this form of wheel, inasmuch as each wheel is practically a portion of a screw with as many threads as there are teeth.

DUPLEX OR TWIN BEVELS.

ART. 128.—No. 5, Drawing P, exhibits another method of effecting the same object by interposing between the driver and follower a double bevel wheel c; and, although more complex, it is better adapted for mill-gearing than either of the preceding arrangements.

WORM AND WORM WHEEL.

ART. 129.—A fourth arrangement for communicating motion to an axis at right angles to, but not in the same plane as the driver, is by means of a worm or endless screw.

When a screw is mounted on a rotative axis, as at Fig 36, it is called an *endless screw* or *worm*, and is com-

Fig. 36.

monly employed for driving a wheel. It very rarely happens that a wheel is employed for driving a worm, although an arrangement of this kind will be found in the mechanism of a common musical box, where the helical axis of the fly or regulator is driven by a wheel of almost infinite breadth. This, however, is quite an exceptional case; the fact of a single-threaded screw being driven by a wheel may be considered as the *wheel and worm paradox*.

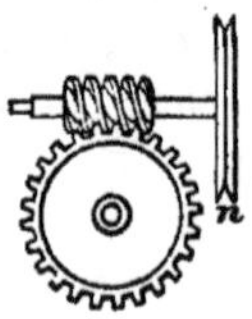

ART. 130.—There are several applications of the screw or worm which it may be interesting to notice. In the first place, the worm is employed by Messrs. Platt Brothers and Company, of Oldham, for driving the spindles of certain slide lathes, on account of its equable motion; for this purpose the worm shaft is driven at about 900 revolutions per minute. The reason for this high velocity will be understood when it is remembered that with a single thread one tooth only of the wheel passes the line of centres for one revolution of the worm; consequently a wheel of 50 teeth would make one revolution only for 50 revolutions of the worm; but with a double thread, two teeth of the wheel will pass the line of centres for one revolution of the worm.

ART. 131.—This slow motion of the wheel and mechanical power of the worm, which is in the ratio of the number of teeth to the number of threads and length of lever,* has been taken advantage of and applied in a most ingenious manner by Mr. John Ramsbottom, of Crewe, for hoisting and carrying about locomotive engines of 25 to 30 tons in weight; the motive power being a soft cotton cord of not more than $\frac{4}{8}$ths of an inch in diameter. This tiny cord, by means of guide pulleys, is made to travel about the erecting shop at the rate of nearly 60 miles an hour, and in every required direction of the travelling cranes, which, as well as the "crabs" for hoisting, are driven by the friction of contact of the cotton cord, which on being deflected so as to press against the periphery of a grooved pulley (n, Fig. 36), keyed on the end of a worm shaft, puts in motion the machinery for lifting the above-mentioned ponderous weights with the most perfect ease, safety, and regularity.

Other beautiful applications of the worm or screw will be found in the adjustments of the microscope, and in

---

* See "Elements of Mechanism," by Mr. T. Baker, Weale's Elem. Series, pp. 76, 77.

measuring the most minute objects and angles by means of the micrometer. For instance, if the pitch of an accurately fitted screw be $\frac{1}{40}$th of an inch, one revolution will cause it to advance that distance. Now, if we suppose the screw to have a circular head or disc, divided into 360 equal parts or degrees, the circular motion of the head of the screw through one degree will give us a lineal measure of $\frac{1}{14400}$ part of an inch.

We have, therefore, in Mr. Ramsbottom's apparatus, a modification, on a large scale, of the most delicate and refined instruments that it is possible to conceive.

Problem XXI.

*Required the projection, full size, of a worm 3 inches diameter, and in gear with a wheel of 40 teeth 1 inch pitch.**

Art. 132.—No. 1, Drawing Q, represents the worm and worm wheel partly in section and partly in elevation. Draw B A the axis of the worm, and D C *the line of centres*, perpendicular to A B.   From B, as a centre, describe three concentric semi-circles, to represent the point, pitch line, and root of the thread, as *e, f, g*, making ff' the pitch circle $=$ 3 inches diameter; and from *f, f'*, draw lines parallel to A B : then will $f\,h$, $f'\,h'$ be the pitch lines of the worm. With a radius (6·36 inches) equal to that of the wheel, and from the line of centres C D, describe the pitch circle F E, touching the pitch line of worm in *k*.

If a continuous rotary motion be given to a worm, the thread will appear to advance, and the effect produced on the wheel will be precisely the same as if the worm were

---

* The diameter and pitch of worm happen to be the same as those used by Mr. Ramsbottom.

moved in the direction of its length. We may therefore conceive the worm (as shown in section) to be a wheel of infinite radius, or a *rack*, which suggests the form of tooth *k* for the wheel, and the form of thread *l m n* for the worm.

In the example before us we have adopted the form recommended in ART. 98. That is to say, the faces of the teeth are epicycloids, and the flanks hypocycloids, struck with a generating circle whose diameter is equal to the radius of a wheel of 14 teeth, 1 inch pitch $= 2\cdot228$ inches; the curves *l m*, *m n*, forming the thread, are cycloids, obtained by rolling the same generating circle along the upper and under sides of the pitch line *f h*; the same method being followed in all respects as for a rack and pinion.

We may observe that the thread and teeth of worm wheels are made in all conceivable forms and shapes, from a round to a square top and bottom; we venture to hope, however, that the form here shown will not be unfavourably looked upon, either as regards strength or the action of the thread upon the flanks and faces of the teeth.

Having thus obtained a section of thread and tooth, find the projection of the point *o p q*, and root *r s t*, of the threads, as explained in ART. 167, Elem. Treat.

The teeth of the wheel are, for greater clearness, drawn in section. A correct elevation of each tooth would be that shown by the dotted lines 1, 2, 3 (see tooth F); because the inclination of the teeth to the plane of the wheel is precisely the same as the line *p q* is to the axis B A of the worm, which is equal to 1 inch in 9·42 inches; *p q* being equal to the breadth of the wheel on the face.

ART. 133.—The operations of the student or draughtsman will be greatly facilitated by the use of generators carefully cut out of a piece of cardboard, which need not be more than one-fourth or one-third the circumference

I

of a circle, as shown at *n*, Fig. 37 ; from the same material (cardboard) the pitch circle *p m* of any wheel may be cut

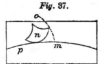

Fig. 37.

out; and all the edges should be rubbed with chalk. The convex and concave edges of *p m* may now be applied alternately to the pitch circle, and the form of curve obtained by carefully rolling the generator *n* along the edge corresponding with the pitch circle, and at the same time dotting off with a fine pointed pencil the curve *m o*, for the face of tooth ; the centre, *p*, of which may be found by trial, and a radius, *p m*, obtained for the required curve; and so on for the flank. In this manner the writer has prepared generators for all pitches by ART. 95 ; and he finds this way of obtaining the form of tooth to be much less troublesome than any of the methods hitherto proposed, and to give results that are not inferior to the best known form of tooth : he presumes, therefore, to designate the adoption of complete sets of generators as *the universal epicycloidal system.*

CHAPTER XI.

ECCENTRICS, WEIGH SHAFTS AND LEVERS, CAMS, HEART WHEELS, WIPERS, TAPPETS, AND RATCHET WHEELS.

ART. 134.—An eccentric may be in the form of a wheel or of a plain disc of metal, through which a hole is bored at any given distance from its centre to receive the shaft on which the eccentric is to be keyed. Therefore the distance from the centre of shaft to the centre of eccentric is called the eccentricity; and twice the eccentricity equals the amount of *throw*, or, in other words, the amount of rectilinear motion the eccentric is capable of producing on a moveable piece called the eccentric rod. See B B′, No. 1, Drawing R, which represents a side elevation and transverse section of an eccentric suitable for a crank shaft 8½ inches diameter; the drawing of eccentric No. 1 being made to a scale of ¾ of an inch to 1 foot.

PROBLEM XXII.

Required the form of eccentric for a shaft 8½ inches diameter, the throw of eccentric being 8 inches. Scale 1¼ inch to 1 foot.

ART. 135.—Draw the centre line A B, No. 1, Drawing R, and from any convenient point C, with a radius of 4¼ inches, describe the circle *b a*. Set off *a e* equal to the thickness required for the boss; and with C *e* as radius, describe the circle *e f* to represent the boss. From C set off the amount of eccentricity in *b* = 4 inches; and from *b* as a centre, with any radius greater than *b e*, describe

I 2

the circle A m g, which will represent the flange of the required eccentric. See m'. Again, o being the centre of motion, and b the centre of the eccentric, it is obvious that one half revolution of o would move b to some point a; hence for the *throw* of eccentric we have b o $\times$ 2 = 4 $\times$ 2 = 8 inches.

The eccentric here described is simply a plate or flat disc with a boss on one or both sides. In large eccentrics, however, it is desirable to reduce the weight by making them in form of a wheel with one arm A f, the rim being strengthened by a web (ART. 50), as clearly shown in our illustration, the section being taken through the line m p. The semi-rings m n, generally of brass, are made to fit accurately in the grooved periphery of the wheel; which groove may be of a convex form, as shown at m', or it may be square with a flange on each side. P P$'$ are the stay rods, with screwed ends for retaining the rings and preventing vibration of the centre rod, to which they are bolted at B$'$; the opposite end of the rod is fitted into a socket or boss B, cast on the semi-ring m g, and firmly secured with a cotter.

The application of the eccentric to working the valve of a steam engine by the intervention of a "weigh-shaft" (sometimes called a rocking shaft) and levers, will be understood from the diagram No. 2, Drawing R; but in order to avoid a mistake sometimes met with in the disposition of the levers b s, s d, we must direct attention to the following general proposition for all levers of rocking shafts.

ART. 136.—*From the centre of rocking motion,* s, *No.* 2, *Drawing* R, *draw a line perpendicular to the rectilinear motion of connecting rod; and the line thus obtained will be the position of lever when at half stroke.*

Thus let a b, c d represent the centre lines of rectilinear motions, and s the centre of rocking motion. Draw b s perpendicular to a b, and s d perpendicular to c d; then will d s, b s be the positions of levers at half stroke. Also,

from s as a centre, with s *b*, s *d* as radii, describe arcs of
circles upon which the quantity and direction of rectilinear
motion can be geometrically projected, as shown by dotted
lines; all the angles at s, the centre of motion, being
equal.

Cams.

ART. 137.—Cams, sometimes called cam wheels, for
changing the direction and velocity of motion, are of
such endless variety that we can do little more than give
general directions for their construction. The regularity
and precision with which cams and tappets are made to
perform their work can be realized only by those who
have had an opportunity of watching the "manipulations"
(if we may so speak) of the "card setting machine," in
which the number and delicacy of movements performed
by what is called "the cam shaft" must be seen in order
to be appreciated.

We remember having heard a proverb, that "every-
thing would be performed by steam except preaching and
card setting." The latter, however, has long been accomplished; and the former, it may be said, is quite within
the range of possibility. In Professor Faber's "Euphonia"
or speaking machine (exhibited at the Egyptian Hall,
Piccadilly, in August, 1846), by operating on a pair of
bellows with the foot, and some two octaves of keys with
the hands, articulate sounds, words, and sentences, in
French, German, and English, were produced; the per-
formance concluding with a musical intonation of our
National Anthem, in which every word was most distinctly pronounced, including the aspirate. Those who
remember this extraordinary machine can quite understand that the row of keys and bellows could be worked
in the same manner as a barrel organ, and so "preach a
short sermon by steam!" In place of a barrel we might
suggest, for a long discourse, the "Jacquard" apparatus

used in figure weaving, which could no doubt be successfully, if not profitably, employed to work the keys of this machine, the inventor whereof informed the writer that his greatest difficulty was with the letter H, and he only succeeded after some twenty years of labour.

ART. 138.—The geometrical construction of cam wheels will be understood from the following explanation, reference being had to the figures on Drawing R:—Let a No. 3 be the centre of a cam wheel $b\,c'\,a$, and let it be required to move a sliding piece b, which we will call the follower, with uniform velocity through a given space $b\,c$ during one-third of a revolution of the wheel. Divide $b\,c$ into any number of equal parts in points 1, 2, 3, c. Set off $b\,e$ equal to $\frac{1}{3}$ of the circumference of wheel; and divide the arc $b\,e$ into the same number of equal parts as the right line $b\,c$, in points f, g, h. From a, the centre of wheel, draw radial lines through h, g, f, e; and make $h\,1' =$ the vertical $b\,1$; $g\,2' =$ the vertical $b\,2$; $f\,3' = b\,3$; and $e\,c' = b\,c$. If a convolute curve be now drawn through points $1', 2', 3', c'$, it will give the form of cam required, because the radial $a\,c' = a\,c$, and $a\,3' = a\,3$, &c.; consequently the points $1', 2', 3', 4'$ of the cam or driver will, during one-third of a revolution, coincide with the points 1, 2, 3, c of the follower, and a uniform motion from b to c will be the result.

ART. 139.—If it were required to give an accelerated or retarded motion to the follower, the line $b\,c$ would have to be divided according to the law of acceleration or retardation, and the curve $1'\,2'\,3'\,c'$ drawn as already described.

HEART WHEEL.

ART. 140.—The object of this form of wheel is to convert a constant rotary motion into a uniform alternating rectilinear motion. This kind of wheel is employed in giving motion to the bobbin-rail in spinning frames, so as

to wind the thread uniformly from end to end of the
bobbin or reel.

The geometrical construction of a heart-wheel is as
follows, reference being had to No. 4, Drawing R:—From
any point A, in the right line e e′, describe a circle a g i,
to represent the boss of the wheel. Set off a e equal to
the amount of rectilinear motion of the sliding piece or
follower, and divide it into any number of equal parts,
say four, in b, c, d. Divide each semi-circumference of
the boss into the same number of equal parts in f, g, h, i;
through which draw, in both directions, radial lines A b′,
A c′, A d′, and make them equal in length to A b, A c, &c.,
which may be effected by describing from A, as a centre,
arcs of circles to cut the radials, as shown by construction.
If a curve be now drawn from a through points b′, c′, d′
to e′, and the same repeated on the opposite side of the
centre line, it will give the form of wheel required, when
the follower moves in a right line.

ART. 141.—When the follower is required to move
through an arc of a circle, the mode of treatment will be
as follows:—Let A B, No. 5, Drawing R, represent a
jointed lever, moving freely upon A as a centre; and let
it be required to move the end B through the arc B c, in
such manner that B will move through *equal vertical
heights in equal times*, from the position A B to the position
A c, by means of a cam acting on a stud or fixed point B
attached to the end of lever A B. Also, let it be required
to raise the lever to the position A c, in the same time
that the axis of the cam makes half a revolution; that is,
while the point d moves to B, in the direction of the
arrow.

From point c draw the right line c r through h, the
centre of driver; from h, with h B as radius, describe the
circle B f m; from B draw B c′ parallel to c h; and from
c draw c c′, perpendicular to c h. Divide B c′ into any
number of equal parts, say four; draw lines parallel to
c c′, cutting the arc c B in points 1, 2, 3; and from each of

these points draw lines 1 h, 2 h, 3 h, cutting the circle B f d in points i, j, k.

Having drawn the diameter B d, divide the semi-circle B f d into as many equal parts as the line B c', in points 5, 6, 7, 8. Take the distance B i, and set it off from 5 to g; take B j, and set it off from 6 to f; take B k, and set it off from 7 to e; take B l, and set it off from 8 to m. Through the points g, f, e, m, draw indefinite right lines h o, h p, h q, h r; make h $o = h$ 1; h $p = h$ 2; h $q = h$ 3; and h $r = h$ c; and through the points thus found draw the curve B o p q r, which will be the proper form of curve for the cam when it moves in the direction indicated.

That the cam will raise the end B of lever to c during half a revolution will be manifest on a little consideration of the figure. For when point 5 arrives at B, point g will be at i, because 5 g is equal to B i; and when g is at i, point o will be at 1, because h $o = h$ 1. In like manner it will be seen that when point 6 arrives at B, point f will be at j, because B $j = 6$ f; therefore p will have arrived at 2 in the arc B c; and so on for the other points.

If the wheel turn in a contrary direction to that indicated, the semi-circle must be divided, as before, into the same number of equal parts as the line B c'; from each of these parts, in the direction of m B, set off the distances B l, B k, B j, B i, commencing at the point d; and draw the radials h r, h s, h t, &c., equal in length to h c, h 3, &c., as shown at r, s, t, u, which will give the proper form of curve when the driver revolves in the direction r s t B; consequently the curve u t s r will produce the same effect on the lever A B, when going in one direction, as the curve o p q r when revolving in the opposite direction.

NOTE.—The arc B c will not be divided equally, because the condition was to raise the end B of the lever through *equal vertical heights in equal times;* a result which would also be obtained by dividing the *chord* of the arc B c equally, and drawing lines perpendicular to c h, cutting the arc in points 1, 2, 3, which would give to the lever a gradually accelerated motion throughout the stroke.   If a uniform motion were required, it would only be necessary to divide the arc equally, and proceed as above described.

WIPERS.

ART. 142.—Wipers differ from cams in this particular, that the form of curve recommended is always the same, namely, the involute of a circle, which has been fully explained in ART. 60; see also No. 6, Drawing R, in which a is the axis of rotation, b, c, and d the wipers, and e, f the stampers.   A number of wipers are made to project, in the manner shown, from a horizontal shaft, for the purpose of raising stampers or pounders in a vertical direction, and letting them fall by their own weight.   They are employed in fulling mills, oil mills, powder mills, bleaching works, &c.

ART. 143.—A more convenient form of wiper is that shown at No. 7, Drawing R.   It is made of cast iron, with an eye a bored out to fit the shaft, on which it can easily be adjusted and keyed, so that the projecting arm of the stamper will pass between the two side plates b b of the wiper, as will be understood.

TAPPETS AND RATCHET WHEELS.

ART. 144.—The distinguishing feature between a tappet and a cam would appear to be that the action of the former is more intermittent, *i.e.*, more like a *tap* or *blow*.   Tappets are extensively used for actuating the treadles of power-looms, and for this purpose they assume an almost endless variety of shapes.

An illustration of the action of a tappet in a simple form

is shown in Fig. 38, which represents a ratchet wheel with
its serrated or saw-like teeth for producing an intermittent
rotary motion of the axis *a*.   *b* is a click, jointed on the

Fig. 38.

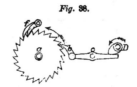

end of a lever, which moves freely on an axis *c*, so as to
allow the click *b* to slide over one or more of the teeth of
the wheel and then drop into an angular space.   D is the
tappet, mounted on an axis, the rotation of which causes
the tappet to strike against and depress the outer end of
the lever, and so raise the click *b*, which drives the wheel
onward; the recoil being prevented by a *detent f.*

A modification of this arrangement as applied to the
cloth-beam of a power loom is called the " taking-up
motion," because it takes up the cloth as the process of
weaving goes on; the amount of motion being very small,
however, it is necessary to have a fine pitch for the wheel,
and three or more clicks, and the same number of
detents, set in advance of each other, so as to divide the
pitch into three or more parts; the intermittent motion of
the wheel can in this manner be reduced to a fraction
of the pitch.   The accompanying figure shows one click
only and two detents.

CHAPTER XII.

COUPLINGS, PLUMBER-BLOCKS, BEARINGS FOR SHAFTS, PULLEYS, &C.

Couplings are employed for connecting the ends of shafts, so as to form a continuous length.

HALF-LAP COUPLING.

ART. 145.—This description of coupling, represented at Fig. 39, consists in forming the ends of two shafts into semi-cylinders; the projecting end of each being made to fit into the recess of the other; and the cylindrical form thus produced is covered with a ferrule, firmly secured by driving in a key. This form of connection, although elegant, is now almost obsolete; a less expensive and much better form is that known as the "muff coupling."

Fig. 39.

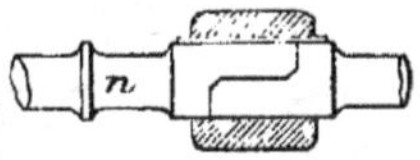

MUFF COUPLING.

ART. 146.—In this form of coupling, $b\ b$, Fig. 40, is a cast iron ferrule or "muff," bored out, and the enlarged

Fig. 40.

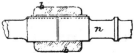

ends of the shafts accurately turned to fit it. A key-way is sunk in each shaft to the same depth as in the "muff,"

which is forced over the two ends, and the whole firmly
secured by driving in the key.

BOX COUPLING.

ART. 147.—Another form of coupling, exhibited at
Fig. 41, consists of two cast iron plates *e e*, *f f*, each
having a boss for keying on the end of the shaft. The
plate *e e* is formed with two segmental openings (see
Fig. 42, which is a face view of the box,) that receive

Fig. 41.   *Fig. 42.*

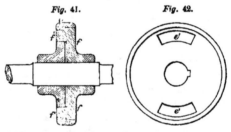

corresponding projections *f' f'*, cast on the face of the
plate *f f*, as shown in section. The rim of plate *e e* is
made to overlap the circumference of plate *f f*, so that the
shafts are retained in a concentric position. To prevent
a twisting strain on the neck of the shaft, the several
parts of this coupling require accurate adjustment, which
adds to the cost; and, being less compact than the muff
coupling, it is now seldom used.

FRICTION COUPLING.

ART. 148.—Fig. 43. This is a combination of discs *a*
and *b* with an annular plate or ring *c c*. Between the discs
a and *b* and the plate *c c* are interposed rings or segments
of leather soaked in grease, which, on screwing up the

bolts, are tightly pressed between the discs *a, b* and plate
e, so that the coupled shaft is driven by the friction of

Fig. 43.

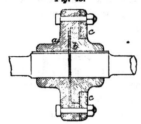

contact of the surfaces. The object of this arrangement,
of which there are several kinds, is to prevent breakage
by the sudden stoppage or starting of heavy machinery.
The driving power will simply depend on the tightness
with which the bolts are screwed up, and can only be
determined by direct experiment; the screwing-up will
therefore require attending to as the frictional resistance
is found to be insufficient.

CLUTCH BOX.

ART. 149.—Fig. 44. This is an arrangement for connecting and disconnecting at pleasure the driven and

Fig. 44.

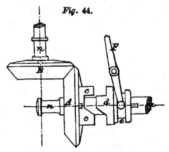

driving parts of a machine, or line of shafting, during the
continuous motion of the driving shaft. Let *n a* be the

driving shaft, A the driving wheel, and B the follower. In the boss of wheel A there are two recesses (diametrically opposite), each having a square and an inclined face c c; d is a clutch with projections corresponding to the recesses c c. Now the shaft n a is made to revolve freely within the boss of wheel A; consequently, in the position shown, the wheels A and B will remain quiescent, notwithstanding the rotary motion of the shaft. Again, the clutch d e is, by means of a sunk key, made to rotate with the shaft, but is free to slide in the direction of its length. F is a lever, terminating in a *fork*, with two studs or cylindrical projections fitting loosely in a groove e. Therefore, on moving the handle of lever to the right, the revolving clutch will slide on the shaft and be "thrown into gear" with the wheel A, and rotary motion will be thus given to B.

Suppose the motion of driving shaft a n to stop suddenly, or to be reversed, the *vis viva* of A and B would cause the inclined planes c to force the clutch into the position shown, and the wheels A B would be free to continue in motion.

When the load on shaft B is considerable, the sudden shock caused by throwing into gear is in effect similar to the blow of a hammer, and therefore detrimental to the machinery; hence the object of friction couplings and friction bands, as described in ARTS. 148 and 150.

FRICTION BANDS.

ART. 150. Friction bands are used for mitigating the injurious effects that attend the ordinary clutch box. The boss of the driving pinion A, Fig. 45, has a groove b, that receives a wrought iron friction band with two "lugs" or projections, or two half rings bolted together so as to be brought into frictional contact with the boss at b; the amount of friction being increased or diminished by tightening or slackening the bolts as may be required.

This clutch is cast with two projections *c c*, that slip over the friction band, and on coming in contact with the

Fig. 45.

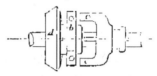

"lugs" or projecting ends thereof the machine is gradually put in motion.   This arrangement is employed for driving " edge runners " and other machines where the resistance from any cause is variable, and frequent stopping and starting unavoidable.

FRICTION CONES.

ART. 151.—If we imagine that part of the clutch marked *c c*, Fig. 45, to be made in the form of a hollow cone, and the boss *b* in the form of a solid cone, and the former to be forced over the latter by means of a lever and screw,—we can understand that A will be driven by the friction of the two coned surfaces, and that the throwing into gear will be attended with less shock and violence than in the clutch-box or friction-band arrangement, the practical difficulty in which is screwing up the bolts to the required amount of tightness.   The proper adjustment of cones is also a matter requiring some attention; care being taken not to make them of such a taper as to stick into and adhere to each other, and yet sufficiently taper to transmit the required power without slipping.

JOURNALS OF SHAFTS.

ART. 152.—The journals, sometimes called *necks*, marked *n n* in the preceding figures, should be turned perfectly true, well polished, and rounded in the angles, as that

form is much stronger than a square shoulder at each end
of the journal. The length of the journal is generally
made *one and a half* times the diameter, which for ordinary mill-wright work ought to be the minimum.

PLUMBER OR PILLOW BLOCK.

ART. 153.—A plumber-block is that portion of a
machine which carries the journals or necks of shafts.
See Drawing S, in which No. 1 is a side elevation, partly
in section; No. 2, an end elevation, with one half in section; and No. 3, a portion of the same in plan In each
of these figures A is the *pedestal*, having projecting feet
for bolting to the frame-work; B the *cap*; and C and D
the *steps*, or *top* and *bottom brasses*, which are bored out
to receive the neck of the shaft. The definitions here
given in italics are those used in the north of England for
the compound parts of that which in the south is called a
plumber or plummer-block.

The difficulty experienced by the young draughtsman
in getting at anything like correct proportions of the
several parts of a plumber-block has induced the writer
to offer the following empirical rule for his guidance.

ART. 154.—Draw a right line $n\ m$, equal in length to
the diameter $b\ e$ of the neck; and divide $n\ m$ into twenty
equal parts for a scale of proportions, or rather dimensions, which are figured on the several parts of No. 1,
Drawing S. Thus, the thickness of the top brass is $\frac{1}{10}$th
of the diameter of the neck $b\ e$, and of the bottom brass
$\frac{3}{20}$ths; the thickness of the *cap* B equals $\frac{4}{10}$ths, and of the
wood packing E $\frac{3}{20}$ths; and so on for the other parts,
which are marked with figures taken from a scale of
tenths and twentieths of the diameter of neck.

NOTE.—In place of making the brasses to fit an octa-
gonal recess, as exhibited at No. 1, they are now generally
made cylindrical, as shown by dotted lines at No. 4;

which figure represents a partial elevation and plan of a more ornamental form of plumber-block, suitable for a 40-horses' power condensing engine, in which the cap is of a circular form, and the brasses cast with lugs *t*, to prevent them turning round within the pedestal.

BEARINGS FOR SHAFTS.

ART. 155.—The common material for the bearings of journals is an alloy of copper and tin, in the proportion of about 10 to 1. This composition, called gun metal, is much harder than common brass, and has hitherto been most extensively used by engineers. Compounds of tin and zinc, with a little copper to harden, have been employed. Pure tin has also been recommended, as producing the least amount of friction with iron; but it is apt to flatten out under pressure, unless confined by a flange or ledge of harder metal, such as cast iron; which combination was the subject of a patent, granted, May 15th, 1843, to Mr. W. E. Newton, to whom the invention was communicated by Mr. Isaac Babbitt, of New York, U.S.

We have known cast-iron journals to run in cast-iron bearings for twelve hours a-day, at the rate of from 1,000 to 1,500 revolutions per minute, with most satisfactory results; the length of journal in this case (the axis of a scutcher beater) being very nearly three times the diameter of the neck; all the parts being carefully got up and kept lubricated with oil. They are now made with self-acting lubricators, *with necks and steps of cast iron.*

ART. 156.—For the bearings of screw propellers Mr. John Penn, of Greenwich, has employed lignum-vitæ with extraordinary results; the only lubrication being a plentiful supply of cold water to carry off the heat. In his experiments on the relative amount of friction of different materials, it was found that a wrought-iron journal, with lignum-vitæ bearings, did not exhibit the least sign of wear (the removal of a slight scratch, for instance), after working thirty-six hours, with a pressure of 1,250 lbs. on the square inch, the velocity being 260 feet per minute at the circumference of the axle.   The result of these interesting experiments * appears to have led to the conclusion that a brass journal, working in hard wood bearings, is, in cases where a constant supply of cold water can be had for keeping the parts cool, practically perfect.

The mode of applying wood for this purpose is to cut dove-tailed grooves in the direction of the length of the bearing, and insert strips of lignum-vitæ, box, or cam wood, which are then bored out to fit the neck of the shaft; a little allowance being made for expansion, and spaces being left between the strips of wood for the flow of water, which acts as a conductor to carry off the heat as rapidly as it is generated.

PULLEYS OR RIGGERS.

The terms pulley and rigger are applied indifferently to a wheel that is driven by a belt or cord.

ART. 157.—When adhesion is necessary, and a cord is employed for driving, the periphery of the pulley is made with a V groove, as shown at K, No. 1, Drawing T. But if the pulley is to act simply as a guide in changing the direction of motion without transmitting power to the axle, as the sheaves of block tackle, &c., the groove is made of a semicircular form, to keep the band in its place, as L, No. 1.

ART. 158.—There is a peculiar property in the action of an endless belt or strap when employed for communicating motion, namely, that of riding upon the largest diameter of the follower. In driving a cone, for instance, a flat belt will tend towards its base; hence the reason for

---

* See " Modern Screw Propulsion," by N. P. Burgh.

rounding the face of a pulley in the centre, as shown at A
and C, No. 2, and 1, 2, No. 5. This swell in the middle of
the follower not only causes a greater amount of adhesion
than an even surface, but tends to keep the belt in its
proper place on the driver B, No. 2, which may have to
carry two or more belts, and is therefore made perfectly
cylindrical. When of this form, it is sometimes called a
drum. It is represented in our illustration as driving the
pulley A' with an *open strap,* and the pulley C' with a
cross strap, which becomes necessary when the direction
of motion requires to be reversed, as indicated by the
arrows. It will also be observed that the belt C C' is
twisted half a revolution in its passage from one pulley to
the other, and that the driving sides of the belt lie flat
against each other at the point where they cross.*

ART. 159.—No. 3, Drawing T, represents the direction
of a belt for communicating motion when the two axes
are in horizontal parallel planes and at right angles. We
have seen this arrangement applied to driving a bench-
drilling machine for light work, and found it to answer
well with a tolerable length of strap and proper adjustment of the pulley E.

ART. 160.—F F', No. 4, Drawing T, represent two
elevations of a pair of guide (vulgarly called gallows)
pulleys. Their object is to divert the direction of motion
of the belt to any given angle, and to communicate motion
to an axis G, which may be either at right angles or
parallel to the driver H. On referring to the front view
F of guide pulley frame, it will be seen that the axes of
the pulleys *i i* are adjustable in slots *g g* to any required
angle within certain limits. The head of the frame, generally bolted to a beam R for overhead motions, may also
be slotted, to admit of its being adjusted bodily.

---

* With two reels of cotton and an endless band of tape, the form
of curves and lines assumed by a crossed strap or belt can be easily
illustrated.

K 2

Although geometrical demonstrations of the angles of such pulleys and direction of motion for straps and bands have been given, we know, from practical experience, that guide pulleys can only be set by a tentative process.

ART. 161.—The arms of light driving pulleys and toothed wheels are frequently made of a curvilinear form, as shown at A′, which is designated the S arm, and at C′, which is called the sickle arm. The curved form, being favorable to deflection, is intended to prevent fracture, which sometimes occurs with radial arms by unequal contraction of the metal when cooling.

SPEED PULLEYS.

ART. 162.—No. 5, Drawing T, shows an arrangement of pulleys for changing the velocity of motion by simply changing the position of the driving belt, which can be moved from one pair of pulleys to another with remarkable celerity and without interrupting the motion of the driver *m m*, which is called the counter shaft; *n n* being the lathe spindle, to which this form of pulley is invariably applied. The velocity of *m m* being constant, that of the spindle *n n* will be in the ratio of the diameter of the pulley driving to that of the corresponding pulley on the lathe spindle, which, according to the position of the strap, is moving at its greatest velocity. In order to change the speed from quick to slower, the right hand of the workman is placed between the open parts of the strap, and by pressing slightly on its edge at *s*, the gathering side, the strap is guided from speed 1 to 2; it will then run loosely on pulley *o*, when, by the slightest touch with the fingers of the left hand at the point *t*, the front gathering side, the strap will be thrown on to the pulley *p*, and the speed of *n n* decreased.

In light lathes, many of which require frequent change of speed, the counter shaft should be brought *within* 5 feet of the lathe spindle, so that the belt may be completely under control for changing the speeds without stopping *m m*, notwithstanding it is provided with a fast and loose pulley, as shown at G, No. 4.

PROBLEM XXIII.

Required the projection of a guide pulley with five sickle arms, the axis being parallel to the horizontal plane, but inclined to the vertical plane. Pulley to be 8 inches in diameter, $2\frac{1}{8}$ inches wide, with boss $2\frac{1}{4}$ inches diameter. Scale, half size.

ART. 163.—Describe circles A, B, No. 1, Drawing U, to represent a front elevation of the pulley to scale required. Sketch in the form for one of the arms, as *a b c, d e f*, and proceed to find, by trial, centres for the curves. If concentric circles be now drawn through the centre points of the curves, and each circle be carefully divided into five equal parts, centres for the curves of each arm will be thus obtained; and the curves may be drawn with a bow pencil.

Let *a f* represent a transverse section of the arm, and *l m* a section, showing the thickness of arm at that point where it joins the rim. Find the horizontal projection, C D E F, No. 2, of the pulley, also the horizontal projection, C′ D′ E′ F′, No. 3, with the axis G′ H′ at any given angle to the intersecting line I L; bisect C F, C′ F′, and draw the centre lines *o p, o′ p′*.

On referring to the form of sections *a f* and *l m*, No. 1, it will be manifest that the points *a, b, c, d, e, f*, will each lie in a plane that coincides with the centre line *o p*, the plane of the arms. Therefore, if from points *a, b, c*, &c., lines be drawn perpendicular to I L, cutting *o p* in points 1, 2, 3, and these points be transferred to *o′ p′*, as 1′, 2′, 3′, —their projection in space will be found by drawing lines from a, b, c, No. 1, parallel to I L., and from $1'$, $2'$, $3'$, No. 3, perpendicular to I L. The intersection of these lines in No. 4 will give the projections of points for the curve $a\ b\ c$, as shown by construction lines for the first point a.

Also any number of points in the curves l', m' (represented by dotted lines), No. 4, can be found in like manner, as explained in Problem XXVI., Elem. Treat.

NOTE.—The student will avoid much confusion in the multiplicity of points and lines in No. 2 and No. 3, by attending to the following instructions:—Take a slip of note paper, and draw a line down the middle, which we will call G^2 H^2; then draw a second line at right angles to the first, say half an inch from the end of the slip, which we will call o^2 p^2. If the loose slip be now applied to No 2, so that the lines thereon correspond with G H, $o\ p$, the points a, b, c, can be projected above the line o^2 p^2 on the loose slip, and the points d, e, f, below, so that one series of points can readily be distinguished from the other, as shown at $x\ y\ z$, obtained from the arm B. The loose slip, with its projected points for one arm, may now be shifted from No. 2, to correspond exactly with G' H', o' p', No. 3; and the points thus obtained can be projected on No. 4. This plan will be found less troublesome, and much more accurate, than transferring with the compasses so many points from $o\ p$ to $o'\ p'$.

The curves of intersection with the boss are found by assuming a thickness for the arm at that point the same as at the rim $l'\ m'$.

CHAPTER XIII.

The Projections of Shadows.

Art. 164.—Notwithstanding that by orthographic projection we are enabled to lay down, on paper, the forms of solids and other figures in such a manner as to render them as intelligible as if the model itself were before us—the projection of shadows and employment of colours are equally important in defining the configuration and material of objects in simple projection. For instance, a cylinder, a prism, or a flat surface, in outline drawing, could not be distinguished one from the other without a plan or section, which is not always convenient; but with the aid of tints, the simple outline assumes the appearance of a solid; and, with the assistance of shadows, its relative position to other objects and the planes of projection can be most clearly defined.

The source of light with which we shall have to deal is the sun, whose rays, on account of his immense distance from the earth, may be considered as parallel and (for the present) to make an *apparent* angle of 45° with the intersecting line of the two planes of projection; because, this projected angle of 45° will not only be found the most convenient for our purpose, but also the most useful in practice: hence the reason for its being adopted as *the rule*. The exceptions are in scenographic delineations, where *effect* takes precedence of *utility*; consequently the direction in which the light is admitted to such representations, as well as the angle, are matters of taste·to be left to the artist.

Art. 165.—In orthographic projections the rays of light, as explained in Chapter V., Elem. Treat., are sup-

posed to come over the draughtsman's left shoulder, and
to strike the upper and lower planes at an angle of
35° 16'. Now the projection of this particular angle of
the rays upon the vertical and horizontal planes will, as
already stated, be in lines drawn at an angle of 45° with
the intersecting line; but the angle which such a ray of
light makes with the intersecting line is 54° 44'. Let us
endeavour to make these matters clear before we proceed
with the shadows.

The Angle of Light in the Orthographic Projections of Shadows.

ART. 166.—If the student apply the set square of 45°
to the edge of the **T** square, and draw two lines A *c*, *a c*,
Fig. 46, they will correctly represent the *projected* angle
and direction of a ray of light in the two planes of projection, of which I L is the intersecting line.

Upon *a c* describe a square 1 2 3 4, to represent the
horizontal projection of a cube; and find the vertical projection 1' 4 7 5 upon the line A *c*. Conceive the line *a c* to
be a plane perpendicular to the plane of projection, and

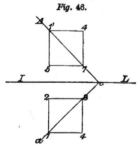

Fig. 46.

a line upon that plane to
enter the cube at the upper
angle 1, and to emerge at
the opposite lower angle
beyond point 3. Such a
line, the longest that can be
drawn within a cube, will
be that which represents
the angle and direction of
an orthographic ray of light
in the horizontal plane.

Again, the vertical projection of the same ray will enter
the cube 1' 4 7 5 at the point 1', nearest the eye, and emerge

at the angle ɣ, which is the farthest from the eye. Therefore A c, is the vertical, and a c the horizontal projection
of a ray or line of light.

PROBLEM XXIV.

*Required the angle which orthographic rays of light make
with the two planes of projection, when the apparent
angle is 45°.*

ART. 167.—*Solution* 1.—From any point c, No. 1,
Fig. 47, draw the vertical and horizontal projections of
the rays c a, c A, at an angle of 45° with I L. From any
point A, in the horizontal ray, draw a line perpendicular

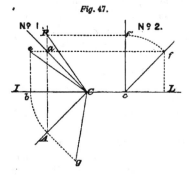

Fig. 47.

to I L, cutting the vertical ray in point a: then will a be
the vertical projection of A. Conceive A C to be a plane
perpendicular to the lower plane, and capable of moving
on an axis at c, and the plane with its ray to be moved
into position c b. Find the vertical projection of b, by
drawing a horizontal line from a to meet the vertical line
from b in e; join e c: then will e c b be the angle which

the ray of light A C makes with the horizontal plane, namely, 35° 16'.

Solution 2.—Perpendicular to A C draw A *g*. Now the height of A above the horizontal plane is equal to *b e*; therefore make A *g* equal to *b e*, and join *g c*: then will *g* C A equal the angle 35° 16',* which the ray A C makes with the horizontal plane. The angle with the vertical plane being the same, can be found in like manner.

--- --- --------- --- -- --

PROBLEM XXV.

Required the angle which the ray of light makes with the intersecting line of the two planes.

ART. 168.—Perpendicular to I L draw *f' c*, No. 2, Fig. 47, to represent an edge view of the vertical plane; from *c* draw *c f*, the luminous ray, at an angle of 45° with the two planes of projection *f' c*, *c* L; and from any point *a*, in the ray *a* C, No. 1, draw a line parallel to I L, cutting ray No. 2, in *f*: then will *f* and *a* represent two projections of a point in space. If we now imagine the ray *c f* to turn on *c* as an axis, the intersection of point *f* with the vertical plane will be *f'*, and a front elevation of *f'* will be F; which is obtained by drawing a vertical line from *a*, No. 1, to intersect the horizontal line drawn from *f'*, No. 2. Join F C: then will F C *b* represent the angle which the rays *a* C, *f c*, make with the intersecting line I L of the two planes of projection. It therefore follows that the angle F C *b* = 90° — 35° 16' = 54° 44'. ·

---

* The radius is to the tangent of inclination of rays as $\sqrt{2} : 1$. Therefore, taking the radius as unity, we have for tangent $\dfrac{1}{\sqrt{2}} = \cdot 7071072$, or logarithm $\overline{1} \cdot 8494852$, which corresponds, within a small fraction, to 35° 16'.

EXAMPLES IN THE PROJECTIONS OF SHADOWS.

Example 1.—To find the shadow cast on the vertical or horizontal plane by a small rod projecting at right angles therefrom.

ART. 169.—Let *a*, Fig. 48, be the point in the vertical plane from which the rod projects, and *a′ c* its plane. If an indefinite line be drawn from *a* at an angle of 45°, as already explained, it will give the direction of the shadow on the plane; and, se-

Fig. 48.

condly, if a line, at 45°, be drawn from *a′*, its intersection with I L will indicate the point at which the shadow touches the vertical plane. Therefore draw *a′ e* at an angle of 45°; and from the point of intersection *e* draw *e f* perpendicular to I L: then will *a f* be the shadow of the rod *a* on the vertical plane.

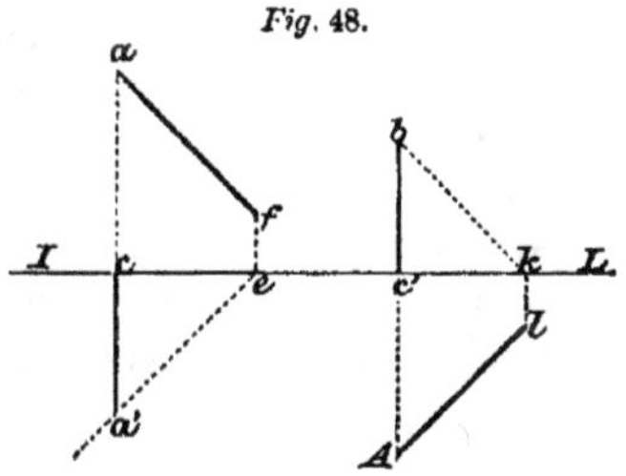

NOTE.—It must be remembered that the intersecting line not only represents a *plan* of the vertical plane, but also an *elevation* of the horizontal plane; a little attention to Nos. 1 and 2, Fig. 47, will make this quite clear.

Example 2.—To find the shadow of a rod on the horizontal plane.

ART. 170.—Let A, Fig. 48, represent the position of rod, and *c′ b* its vertical height. Draw the rays *b k*, A *l*; and from *k*, the point of contact with I L, let fall a vertical line *k l*, which will determine the length of the shadow A *l*.

Example 3.—To determine the shadow cast on the upper plane by a plane which is perpendicular to the plane of projection.

ART. 171.—Let *b c*, Fig. 49, represent the amount of projection of *a b* from the vertical plane. Project the ray

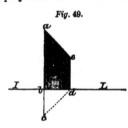

Fig. 49.

c d; and draw *d e* perpendicular to I L to intersect the ray *a e*: then will *b d e a* be the cast shadow. Further, *c d* being the diagonal of a square or cube, of which *b d* and *b c* are two sides, it follows that the breadth of the shadow *b d* is equal to the projection of *a b* from the vertical plane, because *b d* equals *b c*. Therefore the projections in the elevation of a building are thus made apparent without the aid of a plan or section; and for this purpose the projected angle of 45° is not only useful but convenient.

Example 4.—To project the shadow cast by a triangular prism on a plane at right angles to the axis of prism.

ART. 172.—Let 1 2 3, No. 1, Fig. 50, be the end elevation of a triangular prism, and 1′ 4 5 3′ a plan. Find the

Fig. 50.

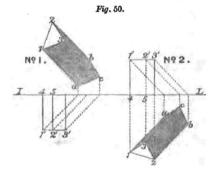

projections of the shadows of points 1, 2, 3 upon the vertical plane, as hereinbefore described, in points a, b, c; join $a\ c$, $c\ b, b\ 2$, and $a\ 1$: then will 2 $b\ c\ a\ 1$ be the shadow required. It will likewise be seen that $a\ c$ is the shadow cast by line 1 3; and $c\ b$ of line 3 2. Also, the line of shadow $b\ 2$ is produced by the projecting angle 2, represented in plan by 5 2$'$; and the line of shadow $a\ 1$, by the solid angle 1, shown in plan by line 4 1.

Example 5. ART. 173.—No. 2, Fig. 50, illustrates the projection of the shadow cast by the same object as in Example 4 upon the lower plane, in which corresponding letters of reference are used, and by substituting the word plan for elevation, and horizontal for vertical, the same description will apply. It is therefore unnecessary to recapitulate what has been said of No. 1; and we would also remark that it is not our intention to append a full description with the tiresome but unavoidable symbols to every example, but to leave the student in some measure to his own resources. So far as we have proceeded, we have endeavoured to explain the lines of construction for obtaining the projected shadow of a *point* or a *line*; and the shadow of a complex figure is nothing more than an application of the principles laid down, which are precisely the same to the end of the chapter. The student is therefore earnestly requested to work for himself, to examine the construction lines, and to trace the cast shadow from point to point, and from line to line, as in No. 1, Example 4, until the projection is complete; remembering that the whole mystery lies in a knowledge of the projection of a point or line upon a given plane or surface, which we will endeavour to make clear with as much brevity as is consistent with the nature of the subject. We consequently recommend the student to place a temporary covering (*i. e.*, slips of paper) over the following figures, 51 and 52, and proceed to work out each example before consulting the figure to which it refers, or reading the text.

Example 6.—To determine the shadow of a rectangular plate upon a vertical plane, when the plate is at any given angle with the vertical, but perpendicular to the horizontal plane.

ART. 174.—Fig. 51. Let A B represent a plan of the plate, and the required angle with I L. Find the elevation 1 3 4 2 of plate, and project the shadows of 1 3 4 2 in *a b c d*, as before described; join *a b, b c,* &c., and the required shadow upon the vertical plane will be obtained.

Fig. 51.

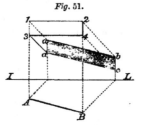

A mere glance at the above figure might almost be considered a sufficient explanation of its construction. It is necessary, however, to direct attention to the rays from A and B. First, the angle of 45° with I L remains the same;—secondly, a single line or ray in the lower plane may represent any number of rays when projecting in the upper plane; and conversely, a single line or ray in the upper plane may represent any number of lines or rays when projecting in the lower plane. Having explained this, we shall leave the *traces of light,** which produce

---

* Trace of light, or " trace of the plane." This expression, although much used in descriptive geometry, is not very generally understood: it means, however, a line left, visible or imaginary, by something passing, or in contact. If the student will fold a piece of paper, and, with his knife, make an incision through the folded edge, then open the sheet to form a dihedral angle (*i. e.,* the angle of two planes), and insert a slip of paper in the incision, he will have a model of the *trace* of two planes, that is, the intersection of two planes with a third plane. The trace of a plane with a cylinder or other solid is the visible or imaginary line of contact with that solid.

the lines of shadow in the next Example, to be defined by the student, who, after completion, can remove the temporary covering and compare his work with Fig. 52.

Example 7.—To find the shadow cast on the vertical plane by a rectangular prism whose axis is parallel to the two planes of projection. The length of prism to be 19 inches; side of square 6 inches. Distance from the vertical plane 8 inches; and from horizontal plane 20 inches. Scale, ½ inch to 1 foot.

ART. 175.—To copy the following or any other figure would be a very simple matter, but to realize those lines or angles which cast a shadow, and those which do not, is not so easy. For instance, the solid angle 1 2, nearest the vertical plane will cast the shadow *a b*; in other words, *a b* is the trace of a beam or plane of rays from that angle. The angle 4 3 will cast the shadow *e f* (see 4′, end view). Again, the horizontal angle represented by 4, will cast the

Fig. 52.

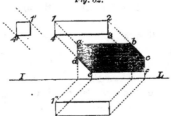

shadow *d e*; and the vertical line 1 4 (see 1″ in plan) will cast the shadow *a d*, &c., &c., as shown by construction.

Example 8.— When the plane of projection is a cylinder, a niche, or a pair of planes making any given angle with each other, the mode of proceeding is as follows :—

ART. 176.— Let No. 1, Fig. 53, represent the elevation, and No. 2 a sectional plan of a concave surface *f g e*, terminating in two plane surfaces *a* and *b*. Now, in order to find the cast shadow of a rectangular plate A B, or other object, on the three planes of projection *a, g e, b,* we have only to assume a number of points, as 3, 4, 5, in any part of the rectangular plate, and find the projection of those points on the concave surface in the same manner as described for a flat surface; which points will give the

Fig. 53.

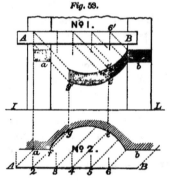

curved form of shadow *g' e',* cast by the upper and lower edges of the plate.

We have said that the points 3, 4, 5 may be taken at pleasure: it is necessary, however, that a ray of light should be drawn from the angle *f,* and produced to *g,* No. 2, in order to determine the starting point of the shadow on the concave surface of the cylinder or niche. For instance, the ray from point 2, after leaving a trace on the angle *f,* will strike the plane of projection in *g,* No. 2, the vertical projection of which is *g',* No. 1. In like manner, a ray drawn from the opposite angle to point 6, No. 2, the elevation of which is 6', will give the terminal points of the cast shadow within the cylinder. The shadows cast by those portions of the plate marked A and B, upon the flat planes *a* and *b* will be understood.

Example 9. ART. 177.—It must not be inferred, from the above, that when the plane of projection is a curve the cast shadow will always be curvilinear, or that the shadow will at all resemble the plane on which it is cast. For instance, the shadow cast by the upper edge of a door, when at right angles to the wall, will be a right line on the jamb-moulding; that being the plane of projection. This is illustrated by Fig. 54, which represents an elevation and sectional plan of a moulding, upon which a

Fig. 54.

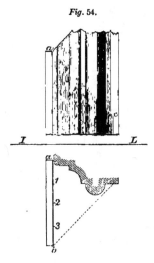

shadow *a c* is cast by a right line or plane that is perpendicular to the vertical plane. Therefore, any number of points, as 1, 2, 3, being taken in the right line *a b*, the projection of those points on the members of the moulding will be found in the right line *a c.* In all orthographic projections of shadows the result will be the same; that is to say, those lines which are perpendicular to the horizontal plane (such, for instance, as the projected shadow of a chimney on the sloping roof and ridge of a building) will be in a right line. This principle is further illustrated by the cast shadow of the ridge, wall, and gable of a

L

dormer-window upon the roof of a house. See Fig. 55, which represents a front elevation of that form of window

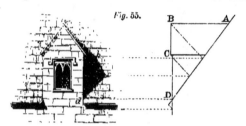

Fig. 55.

with its shadow, the projection whereof will be understood on referring to the diagram A D of sloping roof, the intersection of the rays from B and C with the roof, and the dotted lines of construction. Thus *a b* is the projected shadow of the ridge piece A B; *b c* is the projected shadow of the edge of roof B C; and *c d* the projected shadow of the right-hand angle of the vertical wall, which, like the shadow cast by the vertical angle of a chimney, will be in a line drawn from point *d* at an angle of 45° with the ground or intersecting line, as already explained.

Example 10.—To define the shadow cast by a circular plate.

ART. 178.—When the plane of the circle is parallel to

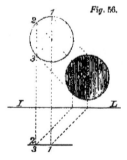

Fig. 56.

the plane of projection, the cast shadow upon that plane

will be a circle of the same radius as the original; hence we have only to find the projection of the centre of the circle, as in Fig. 56, and describe a circle of the same diameter as the original.

The truth of this may be demonstrated by taking any number of points in the elevation, and the same number of corresponding points in the plan, and finding the projection of those points, as shown by 1, 2, and 3. This method must be resorted to when the circular plate is not parallel to the plane of projection; and also when that plane is a cylinder, cone, or other figure, as will be explained.

Example 11.—Given A B C, Fig. 57, the elevation, and *a b c,* a sectional plan of an angular wall,—also 1 5 8, a plan, and 1′ 8′, an elevation of a circular plate, to find the shadow of 1′ 8′ on the wall.

ART. 179.—Divide the circle in the lower plane into *eight* equal parts (which will be found the most convenient number) 1, 5, 7, &c., as shown. Find the vertical projection of 2, 4, 6, in 2′, 4′, 6′. Now, point 2′ is the elevation of 2 and 3 (ART. 174); and point 4′ the elevation of 4 and 5. Also, the horizontal ray from point 1 is in the same plane as 5; from 2 in the same plane as 7; and from 4 in the same plane as 8. Remembering these things —that point 3, in the elevation, is beyond point 2′; point 5 beyond 4′;

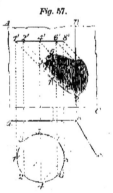

Fig. 57.

and that the projections of the shadow of points 1 and 5 will be in the same vertical plane, inasmuch as they are coincident in the horizontal plane—the projection of the cast shadow on the two planes of projection will be readily found.

L 2

Example 12.—To find the shadow of a circular plate which is perpendicular to both planes of projection.

ART. 180.—Let the right line 1′ 8′ represent an elevation, and the right line 4 2 a plan of the circular plate.

Fig. 58.

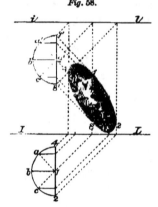

Bisect 1′ 8′ and 4 2; and from each centre 1, 2′, with the radius of plate, describe a semi-circle. Divide each arc into four equal parts in points *a, b, c,—a′, b′, c′* ; and from each of these points draw lines perpendicular to and intersecting the edge of the plate. The result will be a series of coincident points in the two figures. Thus, point 1 is a plan of points 1′, 8′; therefore the projection of the shadows of 1′, 8′ will be 1 and 8. Again points 4, 2 are the plans of 2′ and the point beyond 2′; the projections of their shadows being 4 and 2, as clearly shown. The intermediate points being found in like manner, the elliptical form of shadow 4 1 2 8 will be thus obtained.

ART. 181.—If the intersecting line in the last example be above the elevation, as *i l*, and the rays from points 1′, 2′, 8′, &c., be projected upon that line, we shall obtain the same result as from the plan, which in that case can be dispensed with.

Before proceeding further the student is recommended to vary the foregoing examples, which frequently occur in mechanical drawing, by substituting other planes of projection and simple forms of objects; a practice which will soon lead to a knowledge of the subject, and assist him in that which is to follow.

PROBLEM XXVI.

Required the shadow cast by a round collar on a round shaft, the shaft being horizontal and in elevation.

ART. 182.—Let $a\,b$, Fig. 59, be the elevation of a portion of a shaft, or cylindrical plane of projection, upon which it is required to find the shadow cast by a *collar* or circular disc $1'\,n'$. From any point a, in the centre line $a\,b$,

Fig. 59.

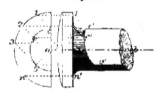

describe two semicircles, representing an end elevation of the visible half of the *collar* $1'\,n$ and *neck* $e'\,g'$. From e, the end elevation, draw the ray $e\,1$. Find the projection of point 1 in $1'$, by drawing a line parallel to $a\,b$; and from $1'$ draw the ray $1'\,e'$: then will e' be the commencement of the shadow.

Again, from any point 2 draw the ray $2\,f$; and find the projection of f in f', as clearly shown by construction. In this manner any number of points in the shadow $e'\,f'\,g'$ may be obtained; observing that the cast shadow will terminate in g', which is the line of separation of light and shade. The position of this line on a cylinder is deter-

mined by the trace of the tangent plane s g; but more
readily still by a line drawn from the centre a at an angle
of 45°, cutting the neck in g and the collar in n; therefore, lines drawn from those points will give the darkest
parts, or lines of separation of light and shade, n' g'. See
Art. 64, Elem. Treat.

PROBLEM XXVII.

*Required the shadow cast by a square cap on a square
column; the column being vertical, with two of its sides at
an angle of 25° with I L; the direction of angle being
from the left, same as the horizontal ray.*

ART. 183.—Let Fig. 60 represent the elevation and
plan of a square prism, surmounted by a square cap; two

Fig. 60.

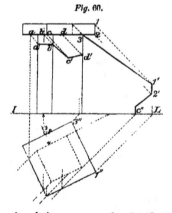

faces of the prism being at an angle of 25° with the intersecting line I L. Now, there is nothing in this problem
which has not been explained in the examples; consequently the solution may reasonably be asked for without
further reference to the text, which will be as brief as

possible in this and remaining problems. First.—*The shadow cast by a straight line on a plane surface will be a straight line; therefore, if the projections of the extreme points in a line be found, the shadow of the original will be a line or plane drawn between those points.* Thus a' b' (Fig. 60) is the shadow cast by line $a\,b$; $b'\,c'$ by the line $b\,c$; and $c'\,d'$ by the line $c\,d$.

Further, as an exercise, the prism may be made a little longer than that shown in the figure, the distance of the plan from I L increased, and the cast shadow of the cap and column projected on the vertical plane. Thus the vertical shadow $1'\,2'$ is obtained from the plan $1''$ and elevation $1\,2$; the line of shadow $3\,1'$ from $3''\,1''$; and the line of shadow $c''\,2'$ from the line $d\,2$.

With a knowledge of the preceding examples, the study of the following shadows may be commenced :—

1. A square cap on a round column;
2. An hexagonal cap on a round column;
3. A round cap on an hexagonal column;
4. A triangular cap on a pentagonal column; together with the projections of their shadows on the vertical or horizontal plane.

The principles being the same in all these examples, the student will find more pleasure in working them out as exercises than he would in reading descriptions which cannot be given without a painful amount of reference and repetition; should any difficulties arise, one or other of the following problems will doubtless remove them.

PROBLEM XXVIII.

Required the shadow cast by a six-sided nut (hexagonal prism) on the horizontal plane.

ART. 184.—The shadow here required is in the lower plane (see Fig. 61), consequently the projections of those points and lines that cast the shadow will be found as explained, ART. 170; that is to say, the ray from any point, as *b*, intersects the plane in *c*, the plan of which is *c′*, &c.

Fig. 61.

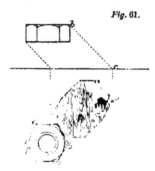

Now there are eight lines or solid angles in this figure, each of which casts a shadow; namely, two vertical, marked *e e*, and six horizontal, which, it is presumed, the student has already found; if not, we may observe that there are three on the upper face of the nut, represented as shadow lines, *e b′ e*, and three on the under face, corresponding to the fine lines *e f e′*. Find, therefore, the projection of the points *e e*, &c., and join them by right or curved lines, as the case may be; remembering, when projecting on a flat plane, that *all lines which are parallel in the original figure, will be parallel in the projection of that figure.* (Art. 90, Elem. Treat.)

<hr />

PROBLEM XXIX.

Given the sectional elevation of a cylinder with a piston midway, in elevation, to find the shadows cast on the concave surface of the cylinder.

ART. 185.—The solution of this problem, and explanation of Fig. 62, will scarcely require us to recapitulate

the projection of any particular ray or rays, which have
already been so fully dwelt upon, that we have purposely

Fig. 62.

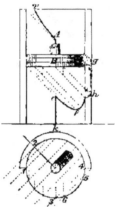

left this figure in outline, in order that some attempt at
the solution may be made before referring to the text,
which will be confined to an explanation of those points
and angles from which the cast shadows are obtained.

Thus, 2', the elevation of 2, will be the point within
the cylinder at which the shadow may be said to commence. The slightly curved shadow 2' A is therefore
obtained from the upper edge of the cylinder, from 2 to
point 1'—see plan. The curved shadow *e f* is obtained
from the lower edge of the piston B; *i. e.*, from point
1 to 3. Again, the line of shadow *g*, on the sectional part
of cylinder, is from the upper edge of piston, from 4 to 5;
whereas *h* is from the lower edge of piston, 3 to 6 in the
plan; and A *e k* is from the vertical edge, marked 1 in
plan, which will be understood. In all examples of this
problem met with by the writer, the shadow *g h* has been
overlooked.

The following problem should be attempted as an exercise before consulting the wood engraving or the text.

PROBLEM XXX.

The vertical section of a cylinder, 1 foot 9 inches internal diameter, has a plain flat cover (also semi-circular) 2½ inches thick; through the centre of cover is a semi-circular concentric opening of 4 inches radius; required the shadow cast by the edge of cover and opening on the concave surface of the cylinder.   Scale, 1¼ inch to 1 foot.

ART. 186.—The solution of this problem is represented in outline by Fig. 63, which may be thus described :—*a b*

Fig. 63.

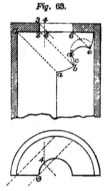

is the cast shadow of line 1 2; *b c* of line 2 3; *c d* of line 3 4; and *d e* of line 5 6.   The dotted lines show the complete projection of the two semi-circles; and the full lines represent the lines of separation of light and shadow.

PROBLEM XXXI.

To find the shadow of the salient angles within the concavity of a niche having a semi-hemispherical head.

ART. 187.—Let Fig. 64 represent the elevation and plan of a *niche; e f g h* being the cylindrical, and *e a f* the spherical part. The projection of luminous rays and shadows within a cylinder having been explained, we have only to direct attention to those rays which fall upon the semi-dome or spherical head of the niche; and for the projection of those rays we shall give two methods.

First method.—Suppose each ray, as A B in the plan, to be a line of section; the vertical projection of such line of section will be a portion of an ellipse (not shown in the drawing). If however such ellipse, or a portion thereof, be found, and also the vertical projection of point A in *a*; then, the intersection of the ray *a b* with the elliptic curve will give a point, namely point *b*, in the line of separation of light and shadow; and in this manner any number of points in the line of the shadow can be found by first obtaining vertical sections of the niche cut by planes drawn parallel to A B.

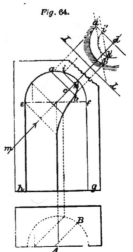

Fig. 64.

This method, on account of the ellipses, is somewhat troublesome; it is desirable, however, to work out one example, that it may more easily be remembered, and the principle applied in cases where it is found convenient.

Second method. — Suppose the two rays *a b*, *i k*, indefinitely produced, to be sectional planes, in each of which there is a line of light making a given angle (35° 16′) with the plane of projection. It will be manifest that the point of intersection of each ray with its sectional plane would become apparent if viewed in the direction of the arrow *m*. Therefore, from the centre of arc *e a f*, draw *c d* perpendicular to *a b* and *i k*; and from any point *d*, with the radii *c a*, *k i*, describe arcs of circles $a'\,b'$, $i'\,k'$, which will represent sections of the spherical head of the niche cut by planes $a\,b$, $i\,k$. If we now suppose I L to be the intersecting line of the two planes of projection, and $a'\,b'$ a ray of light making an angle of 35° 16′ with I L,—b will be the point of intersection of the luminous ray with the section; and the projection of b' on the line of section is b: therefore, b is the point of contact of the ray $a\,b$ with the spherical portion of the niche; and so on for any number of points, of which k, the projection of k', is also a point in the line of shadow.

The shadows cast by the salient angles of sections of domes, groins, &c., are found in this manner.

PROBLEM XXXII.

The plane of projection being a right cone, required the line of separation of light and shade on the surface of the cone.

ART. 188.—Firstly.—Find the horizontal projection of the shadow of the apex of the cone in a, Fig. 65, which will be understood. Draw $a\,b$, $a\,d$, tangential to the base

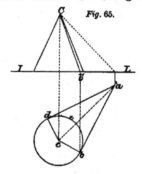

Fig. 65.

of cone; and from c, the centre of cone, draw $c\,b$, $c\,d$, perpendicular to the tangential lines $a\,b$, $a\,d$: then will $a\,d\,e\,b$ be the cast shadow on the horizontal plane, and $b\,c$, $d\,c$ the lines of separation of light and shade on the surface of the cone. The darkest part of the elevation is therefore b' c, the vertical projection of b c.

ART. 189.—Secondly.—When the cone is inverted, as in Fig. 66, the operation is as follows: *

From the apex of the inverted cone draw c a, at an angle of 45°, to meet the plane of the base line of cone prolonged from b''. From a, the point of intersection, let fall a perpendicular, cutting a luminous ray drawn from c in a'; draw a' b', a' d' tangential to the base of cone, and c b', c d' at right angles to the tangential lines. Find the elevation of b' in b'', and join b'' c, which will give the line of separation of light and shade, and therefore the darkest part of an inverted cone.

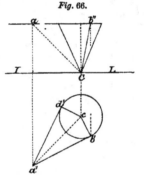

Fig. 66.

A little reflection with a model cone of paper, which the student will know how to make (ART. 162, Elem. Treat.), will sufficiently illustrate the rationale of the lines of separation of light and shade, and the greater amount of illumination in one case than the other will be obvious.

PROBLEM XXXIII.

Required the shadow cast by a right line on the surface of a cone; the line being parallel to both planes of projection.

ART. 190.—This problem is intended to illustrate two methods of determining the point of contact of a luminous

---

* The Author has purposely avoided the use of letters of reference to designate the cone, as it is perfectly clear without those hinderances, which have been used as sparingly as possible.

ray with any part of the surface of a cone or other solid.

The first method is by vertical sections; that is to say, each ray of light is supposed to represent a vertical plane that divides the cone perpendicularly to its base. Thus let E F, No. 1, Fig. 1, Drawing V, be the elevation, and *e f* a plan of the right line of which the shadow is required on the surface of cone; also let it be required to find the point of contact, on the surface of cone, of a ray of light *e c*, which passes through the axis. The vertical section in this case will be an isosceles triangle, and the front or visible leg, *g* C, that on which the ray of light will fall. Now E H is the vertical projection of the ray *e c*; and the intersection H with the section line *g* C is the point of contact of the ray *e c* with the surface of the cone.

The point of contact, H, may also be shown in the manner following:—Let the cone with its points and lines turn upon its axis so that *e c* coincides with *e′ c*. Now the vertical projection of the ray in this position would present an angle of 35° 16′, as shown by *e″ h*. If the cone be moved back again to its original position, the point *h* will coincide with the original point H, which is the projected shadow of *e* and E.

This method of finding the shadow cast by a point in space is applicable whether the plane of projection be a cone, sphere, or other form of solid; but as every section of a cone, parallel to, but not passing through the axis, will be a hyperbolic curve, and the projection of this curve must be found before we can find the shadow of a point, it may be desirable to seek for the remaining points in the foregoing problem by the second and more simple method of horizontal sections. Previous to describing this method, however, we must direct attention to the highest point in the shadow, in order that we may know where to commence with the sectional planes.

ART. 191.—*Highest point in shadow.*—We will once more turn the cone, Fig. 1, Drawing V, on its axis, until the line *c n* coincides with *c n'*; that is, one-fourth of a revolution (see plan). In this position the vertical projection of *n'* will be E. Therefore, from point E draw the ray E *o* (45°); and from *o* draw *o n²* parallel to I L: then will *n²* be the vertex of the shadow. This is exemplified by No. 3 which represents an end elevation of the right line *e f* and also a ray of light. For, whether we view the rays in the direction of the arrow *y*, or the arrow *z*, they still present the same angle of 45°; and the point of contact, *k*, in No. 3, is the same as *n²*, No. 1.

ART. 192.—The second method of determining the point of contact of a luminous ray with the surface of a solid is by horizontal sections; and it consists in finding the projection of certain points in the line of shadow upon the lower plane, and afterwards transferring them to corresponding lines of section in the upper plane. Thus, from any point F in the line E F (No. 1, Fig. 1, Drawing V,) draw the elevation of a ray of light F 3; and from *f*, No. 2, a plan of the same ray. From any point in the ray F 3, draw a line of section 2 2, parallel to the base of cone, and conceive this line to be a plane, in which there is a circular opening of the same diameter as the cone at the point of intersection. From *c*, No. 2, describe a circle, or portion of a circle, of the same diameter as the section of cone cut by plane 2 2. Now, the horizontal projection of the shadow of line *e f* upon this imaginary plane will be 2' 2'; and the points of its intersection with the circular opening at *s s* will give two points in the shadow of right line *e f* on the surface of cone, which is the plane of projection. Find, therefore, the vertical projection of the two points in *s' s''*; and draw the curved line of the shadow H *n²* *s''*. Thus, by a series of horizontal planes, and intersections of the cone, as above described, any number of points in the vertical and horizontal projections of the line of shadow may be found; observing that we lose the cast shadow as it approaches the line of separation of light and shade at *s''* in the upper plane.

PROBLEM XXXIV.

The axes of a cone and sphere, 16 inches apart, are in plane which makes an angle of 50° with the vertical plane. The radius of sphere, 6½ inches, is equal to the radius of the base of cone, whose height is one and a half times the base. Required the vertical and horizontal projections of shadow cast on the surface of sphere; the projected angle of the luminous rays being 45°. Scale 1 inch to 1 foot.

ART. 193.—From any point L, in the intersecting line of Fig. 2, Drawing V, draw L c, making an angle of 50° therewith; and from any convenient point c describe a circle of 6½ inches radius for the base of cone. Make c a equal to 16 inches; from a, with the same radius, 6½ inches, describe a circle to represent a plan of sphere; and find the elevation of sphere and cone in the vertical plane, as No. 1.

From c, the apex of cone, and at an angle of 45°, draw the plan of a luminous ray c b, represented in elevation by c L. Now find the elevation of cone and sphere, No. 2, in a plane, the intersecting line i l of which is parallel to the luminous ray c b. Then each and all of the rays in No. 2 will make an angle of 35° 16′ with i l. Therefore, from c^2, the apex of cone, draw an indefinite ray c^2 e, and find the sectional elevation of sphere cut by the corresponding ray c e' b; and from a' as a centre describe a portion of such section, cutting the ray from c^2 in e, which will be the point of contact or projection of the ray from c^2 on the sphere.

Now, the plan of e is e'; and the vertical projection of e' is e'', No. 1: therefore e'' is the point at which the ray from c would strike the sphere.

Again, c^2 f, No. 2, is the elevation of the two lines of separation of light and shade c f and c f'; and c f^2, c f^3, No. 1, are the vertical projections of those lines,—they are also the lines which cast the shadow. Therefore we have only to find the projection of shadow cast by any number of points in lines c f^2, c f^3, in the same manner

as just described with regard to point c; care being taken
to make all the points in those lines to coincide, which
is best done by dividing the lines $c^2 f$, and $c f'$, &c., into
a given number of equal parts from the apex of cone;
because, if lines were drawn from points in $c^2 f$, to cut $c f$,
or $c f'$, the intersections would form such an acute angle
as to be difficult, if not impossible, to determine.

PROBLEM XXXV.

*The projected angle of luminous rays being the same as in
the preceding Problem (45°), it is required to find the
shadow cast by a sphere on the horizontal plane, and
also the vertical and horizontal projections of the great
circle that casts the shadow.*

ART. 194.—From any point A (Fig. 3, Drawing V), as
a centre, describe the great circle of a sphere so as to
touch the ground line I L; and draw A a perpendicular to
I L. From any convenient point a, draw a plan of sphere
and luminous ray $a b$. Now find the projection of sphere
in plane No. 2, in which all the rays make an angle of
35° 16' with intersecting line $n b'$, which is drawn parallel
to $a b$. Draw the diameter 1' 3', perpendicular to the rays;
and find the projection of 1' 3' in the lower plane, as shown
by the ellipse 1 2 3 4, which is the horizontal projection of
the great circle that casts the shadow $c b e$.

To obtain the vertical projection of the hemisphere, we
have simply to find the elevation of points 1, 2, 3, 4, and, to
ensure greater accuracy, say, of four intermediate points.
Thus, the height of point 1 above the horizontal plane is
equal to $n 1'$; therefore, find the elevation of point 1, in the
upper plane, which is 1''. If a line be now drawn from
1'', at an angle of 45°, cutting the ground line in L, and a
vertical line be let fall from that point to cut the initial
ray, its point of intersection b will be the same as that

M

obtained by drawing a line from b' perpendicular to $a\,b$. It is obvious that points 2, 3, 4, and any number of intermediate points, are to be found in the same way; and the whole will form a very interesting study.

ART. 195.—Fig. 4, Drawing V, represents a hemispherical cup with a bar $a\,c$ laid across. The shadow cast by the cup on the horizontal plane is obtained by two or more horizontal sections, Art. 192. The cast shadow of the edge of cup upon the concavity and also the cross bar are obtained by vertical sections, as explained in Art. 187.

PROBLEM XXXVI.

Required the line of separation of light and shade, or darkest part, of the torus * of a column.

ART. 196.—See Fig. 5, Drawing V. There are four points a, b, c, d, in this figure (see elevation) that present so little difficulty as to require but few remarks; there are others, however, to which we must direct some attention, as a knowledge of the principles of construction once acquired will, in future practice, render the projection of the darkest part of a torus quite unnecessary.

In the first place, points a and d are simply the tangential points of contact of two rays, which may be determined by drawing from the centre of each semicircle a line with the set square of $45°$. Again, point c is manifestly the elevation of the tangential point of contact of the ray H K, determined by drawing the radial line A C at an angle of $45°$ with the axis. Hence we have three points in the line of separation of light and shade on the torus. The fourth point, to which we shall again

---

* The torus is a large semicircular moulding, used for the bases of columns, and differs from the astragal only in size ; the latter being much smaller than the torus.

refer, may be determined by drawing a line from a parallel to I L, cutting the vertical axis in b.

We will now proceed with an explanation of and the mode of obtaining the projection of intermediate points by vertical sections; for this purpose we will designate the line A B the normal section, to which we request attention. In this section we may take *any* point e, and find its elevation in e' by turning the section on A as a centre, as before explained, ART. 190. Join e' A; and parallel to this line draw e'' A', tangential to the torus: the tangential point 1 being determined as described for points a and d. From point 1, let fall a vertical line 1, 1'; and from A as a centre, with A 1' as radius, describe an arc intersecting the normal ray in point 1'', which will be the point of contact of the ray B A with the under side of torus. Now find the elevation of point 1'' in n, by drawing a vertical line from 1'' to intersect a horizontal line from point 1; — n will therefore be a point in the line of separation of light and shade.

In the above manner any number of sections from the normal to section A C can be obtained: that is to say, *by drawing from the given point e, in the normal section A B, a line perpendicular to each line of section &c.* Thus, from the given point e, draw e h, perpendicular to any line of section, as A H. Now find the elevation of point h (by turning the line of section on A as a centre, as before described) in h'; and join h' A. Parallel to h' A draw the tangent h'' A'; from the point of contact 2, let fall a perpendicular 2 2'; and transfer the point 2', as shown by dotted lines, to cut the line of section A H in 3. Now the vertical projection of this point on the torus will be h^3, as described for the point n.

Notwithstanding .that the points and lines we have attempted to describe are never used in practice, the student may discover that the several points e, f, g, h, A, in the plan, are all contained in a semi-circle, of which o is the centre; and he may wish to know the "why and the wherefore" of what he has been doing. The answer is simply this,—the lines e' A, f' A, g' A, h' A, and c'' A *are the vertical projections of the luminous rays as seen perpendicular to each line of section.* For instance, suppose we treat the section A C in the same manner as described for section A H; that is, from point e draw a perpendicular to A C. The result will be a point or line A, the elevation of which will be c'' A. Now, parallel to c'' A draw a tangent to the torus, as shown at p; treat the point of contact as before, and its projection on the torus will be point c, already explained. In other words, the inclination of the line h' A is that which would be presented by any luminous ray, as $s\ t$, if seen in the direction of the arrow H, which is perpendicular to the section A H; in like manner the ray of light B A, if looked at in the direction $g\ e$, which is perpendicular to A G, will present an angle of 45° the same as g' A; and so on for any other line and section.

To find the projection of a point between c and d in the elevation. Make C 4, in the plan equal to C 3: then will the vertical projection of point 4 be just as much above the centre line of torus, or point c, as point h^3 is below that line.

The amount of interest attached to this problem has induced us to give this somewhat lengthy solution, to which we may add that points in the line $a\ b\ c\ d$ of separation of light and shade may be found by vertical sections of the torus cut by the rays, as will be understood from the following problem.

Problem XXXVII.

Required the shadow cast by the corona, or larmier, on the capital of a column.

Art. 197.—No. 1, Drawing W, represents the shadow projected on the colarino, or neck of the capital, of a

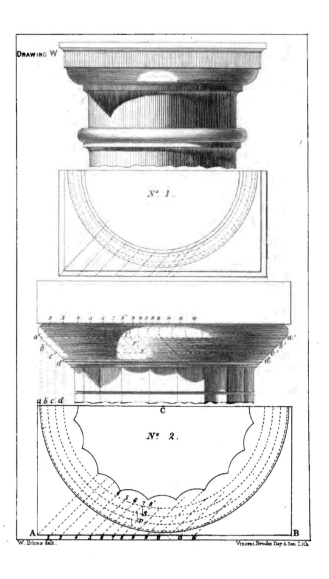

DRAWING W

N.° 1.

N.° 2.

C

A
B

W. Binns delt.

Vincent Brooks Day & Son Lith.

Tuscan column; and No. 2 represents the plan and elevation of a Grecian Doric capital with the shadows projected
and lines of construction.

In the solution of this problem by vertical sections it
will be necessary to find the elevation of a number of sectional planes, cut by rays 5 5, 6 6, 7 7, &c. (see plan, No. 2),
also the vertical projection of the corresponding rays and
their points of contact with the sections, which will give
points in the line of separation of light and shade.

From c, the centre of column, with any convenient
radii c a, c b, &c., describe three or four concentric semi-
circles; and find their elevations in a' a', b' b', &c. From
any point in the corona A B, say point 8, draw a ray 8 r 8 $8'$;
and find the vertical projection of r 8, &c., also the section
of ovolo, as shown by the dotted line t' r' s'. Now, find
the elevation of point 8 in 8''; and from 8'' draw a ray (45°)
cutting the line of section in t': then will t' be a point in
the line of shadow; and so on with any number of sections
and points in the line of separation of light and shade.

ANGLE OF LUMINOUS RAY.

ART. 198.—The angle of 45°, being the most convenient
for illustration and useful in practice, has been adopted
in all the preceding examples, which have been selected
with a view of leading the student to a general knowledge
of a subject that especially requires practice; reading is
not sufficient, nor yet so impressive as working and study,
which in many cases will render a perusal of the text in
some of the problems unnecessary. We must, however,
caution those who are preparing for examination that the
direction and inclination of the rays of light may be
assumed at any other angle, and the question stated
somewhat as follows :—

*Required the horizontal projection of the shadow, &c., &c.,
when the rays of light are in planes which make an angle
of 40° with the vertical, and 27° with the horizon; their
direction being from the right.*

Solution.—The object being a prism or other solid, we
have simply to draw *d e*, Fig. 67, at an angle of 40° with
ı L, to represent the plane and direction of the rays. If
we now assume *d e* to be the intersecting line of another

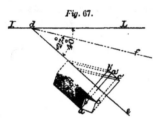

Fig. 67.

plane, and draw *d f* at an
angle of 27° therewith, *d e*
and *d f* will form a di-
recting diagram for the
projection of the shadow
of any object, such as a
prism *a b c*, as will be
clearly seen from the lines
of construction, in which
all the rays are in planes that make an angle of 40° with
the vertical plane, and each ray makes an angle of 27°
with the horizontal plane. In this manner the angles and
subjects may be varied *ad infinitum*.

ART. 199.—Before we leave this part of our course it
may be desirable to point out a track which, if persevered
in, must ultimately lead to success; therefore it is with
this object that we now introduce the reader to a sheet of
studies which were some years since the spontaneous
production of Mr. John S. Rawle (formerly a student of
the author's at the Schools, South Kensington), who, after
passing through a course similar to the foregoing, applied
his acquired knowledge of the principles to the projection
of shadows cast by spheres, cones, pyramids, and prisms
upon one another, some of which are exhibited on the
last sheet of drawing, marked X, which may be useful in
directing the reader's attention to an unlimited number of
examples in the Projection of Shadows.

CHAPTER XIV.

SHADING AND COLOURS.

ART. 200.—The art of embellishing geometrical drawings with colour, or tints, is one that requires a great deal of practice, and, if possible, ocular as well as oral instruction. To see an expert draughtsman manipulate with a couple of sable pencils, accompanied with a few encouraging words of instruction, will do much more for the student than pages of our text, let them be ever so carefully written.

Such instruction, however, although now more conveniently attained than it was before the opening of Science and Art Schools, is not always at hand. It is therefore with a view of assisting the needy in this respect that the writer attempts to lay down a few simple rules and instructions, based on his own practice, for the guidance of those who may be so circumstanced as to be debarred the great advantages of a living teacher.

DEFINITIONS.

1. *Those parts of a body which receive the direct rays of the sun are said to be in* LIGHT.

2. *Those parts of a body which do not receive the direct rays of the sun are said to be in* SHADE.

3. *That part of any surface which is deprived of light, by another body intercepting the sun's rays, is said to be in* SHADOW.

ART. 201.—The most elegantly finished drawings are those in which there is an entire absence of outline, except that which is produced by colour, light tints, shade, or shadow. Consequently the outlines of a coloured drawing, if in ink, should be exceedingly fine. When shading and shadows are employed, *medium* and *shadow lines* (Chapter V., Elem. Treat.) should be omitted.

RULES FOR FLAT TINTS OR WASHES WHEN THE SURFACE IS ILLUMINED.

ART. 202.—1. All surfaces parallel to the plane of the picture, and therefore equally distant from the eye, receive a tint of uniform intensity.

2. Those surfaces which are farthest from the eye receive the darkest tint; the nearest surface being the lightest.

3. Surfaces which are inclined to the plane of the drawing (as the left hand face of pyramid in Drawing X) are to be shaded with a tint of slightly varying intensity; the darkest part being that which is farthest from the eye.

Presuming these simple rules to be committed to memory, it will be easy also to remember that the converse is the case for surfaces in shade.

SURFACES IN SHADE.

ART. 203.—1. All surfaces parallel to the plane of the drawing receive a flat tint, reduced in intensity as the surfaces recede; the nearest to the eye being the darkest, unless influenced by reflected light.

2. Surfaces inclined to the plane of the drawing, and in shade, receive a tint of varying intensity; the *darkest* part being that *nearest* the eye, as the right hand face of pyramid in Drawing X.

3. The tone of a shadow cast on one or more planes should be the deepest on that plane which receives the greatest amount of light.

Experiments with shadows of objects cast on pasteboard planes, with a strong artificial light, will serve to impress the subject on the mind more forcibly than rules, which are less interesting and not so easily remembered as the results of experiment. A blacklead pencil, for instance, if held at an angle of about 45°, with its point touching the plane of projection (sheet of cardboard or paper), will produce a beautifully toned shadow—forcibly illustrating the foregoing rules. The production of such a shadow is termed *shading*, which we shall presently explain.

MODE OF TINTING BY REPEATED WASHES.

ART. 204.—Tinting here implies the covering of surfaces with a flat tint of colour of greater or less intensity, and is most readily accomplished by a number of flat washes, and *stippling*. For this purpose a large brush, capable of retaining a fine point when moderately charged with fluid colour, is to be preferred.

The drawing is prepared by washing the surface with a sponge and clean water, or the part only to be tinted with a brush; in which operation, if care be taken not to go over the boundary lines, there will be less difficulty in keeping to those lines with the colour. If, however, by accident, the boundary should be exceeded, a *clean* finger of the left hand should be *instantly* applied to brush the colour back.

Let the drawing board be placed at an angle sufficient to assist the flow of colour, which should be light; the depth of tone being obtained by repeated washes. Take as much fluid in the brush as can safely be carried (with the brush in a horizontal position) over the sheet without its dropping, and commence at the upper left hand corner, carrying the brush from left to right, then back again; care being taken not to pass the brush a *second time over the same surface during the same wash,* and especially to keep as nearly as possible the same quantity of colour flowing,—a fresh supply being taken in the brush before the preceding one has been spread. In other words, to keep in motion, with the point of the brush, a flow of colour which cannot very well be in excess, except at the termination of the wash, when the overflow must be taken up with a damp brush.

ART. 205.—We may here observe that mechanical draughtsmen do the principal part of their work (large or small) with a couple of sable brushes, attached to the same holder; one for water, and the other for colour; the former being a red sable, and the latter a black one. This distinguishing feature will be useful in avoiding the mistake of putting the water brush into the colour, which might lead to disagreeable results. There is also a greater stiffness in red sable, which renders it peculiarly applicable to the purposes of a water brush.

Repairing Defects with the Water Brush, and by Stippling.

ART. 206.—Notwithstanding the amount of care that may be taken to carry out these instructions, inequalities in the tone and *little* blotches beyond the boundary lines will occasionally make their appearance. With regard to the latter, the only remedy is a brisk application with a lateral motion of the point of the red sable brush with water to wash out the defects; a piece of clean blotting paper being used from time to time to remove the stains and reduce the boundary line to a sharp edge.

ART. 207.—The operation of repairing defects by erasing with a knife should, in all finished drawings, outline or coloured, be avoided as much as possible; if, however, the removal of an ink line be indispensable, we recommend that the coloured drawing should be completely finished (except the defect) before the erasure takes place ; because a wash of colour applied to an abraded surface will leave a stain, which cannot very well be removed, whereas the erased part can be repaired by stippling.

ART. 208.—The process of stippling is performed, not by "gently rubbing," nor yet by brushing, for that would imply painting, but by producing a number of *dots* with the point of a very dry brush, in which there is *an almost imperceptible amount of colour.* The operation although tedious is somewhat fascinating, on account of the soft and beautiful effect produced by a number of minute touches in imitation of dotted engraving ; it will frequently be required in correcting defects in the process of shading.

SHADING.

ART. 209.—By this term we mean a softening off or gradation in the tone of light and colour, as in the hues of the rainbow—a process whereby a circle is made to assume the form of a sphere, a rectangle to represent a cylinder, and a number of parallel lines an elaborate moulding.

There are three methods of shading cylindrical surfaces and drawings generally.

The first method, known as the French system, consists in applying a number of flat washes, commencing at the darkest part of a surface, intended to be cylindrical, with a narrow strip of colour, over which is laid a wider strip ; and so the process goes on wider and wider at every step until the cylinder, when finished, presents the appearance and form of a polygon, rather than a cylinder, upon which a number of meridian lines must be drawn to regulate the breadth of each wash.

ART. 210.—The second method will be found useful in making large drawings for illustrating lectures, &c., on

account of the facility of producing effect. Prepare a
quantity of Indian-ink, thick and black, almost the con-
sistency of cream. With the point of a brush, lay a
narrow strip or thick line of the ink along the darkest
part of all the cylindrical surfaces, previously lined out in
pencil; the breadth of strip being regulated by the diameter
of cylinder. This operation having been performed, and
the parts left to dry, take a wet or rather damp brush and
apply it in such a manner (*i.e.*, by brushing) as to remove
in some measure the sharp edges of the black strips, and
cause the ink to run, or spread slightly over the moistened
surface of the paper. This being done throughout the
drawing, and the shadows projected and washed in, the
process of tinting or washing the surfaces with the required
colours may be commenced; the washes being carried over
the black strips, which will be further reduced in tone by
a portion of the ink being mixed and carried off with the
colour. On a paper of open texture, by dexterous mani-
pulation, a surprising effect may be produced in a remarkably short time; and, with the aid of a little stippling,
and occasional washing with sponge and water, a drawing
of a much higher character than lecture diagrams may be
produced.

ART. 211.—The third method is that employed in the
production of finished drawings of machinery by "softening off." Prepare the surface of the paper by washing
with a brush or sponge and clean water; and commence
with a light shade and narrow strip of colour along the
darkest part of the cylinder to be shaded. Reverse the
brush in the hand, and with the red sable and a little
water take a sweep along one edge of the strip and then
along the other, so as to cause the colour to flow or spread
over that portion of the surface which has been damped
with the water brush. A little practice on a piece of
cartridge paper will dictate the necessary amount of water
for the brush; as if it be too sparingly used, the colour
will not spread sufficiently; and if too copiously used, the

colour will be diluted and rendered uneven. Practice alone must therefore be the guide, not only as regards the quantity of water, but also the quantity and depth of colour, which should be very light to commence with.

Further, we do not recommend that the work should be *perfectly* dry before a succeeding coat is applied,—for this reason, colour will spread more evenly on a slightly damp (not wet) than on a perfectly dry hard surface; care, however, must be taken not to commence a wash until the preceding one has been absorbed sufficiently to prevent a portion of it being removed by a touch of the brush; otherwise a clouded and uneven surface, requiring the tedious process of stippling, will be the result.

The operation of laying on the colour and softening off may be continued and extended until the cylindrical forms assume the appearance shown in Drawings W and X, and also in Drawing L, Elem. Treat.

The flat tints and washes, also, being repeatedly laid over the cast shadows will produce a soft and agreeable tone. If, however, the colours have been used too dark, and the general effect uneven and disagreeable, the whole surface of the sheet may undergo a process of sponging.

Sponging with Water.

Art. 212.—This process is performed with the drawing board inclined, so that the water, which must be very freely used, will flow over the surface, and carry with it the colouring matter removed by sponging. The operation is commenced at the *upper end* of the inclined board, with a soft sponge, which is filled with clean water, and passed to and fro across the sheet; the sponge being replenished as the washing goes on. Confidence and a plentiful supply of water are all the requisites for success in this operation. When the paper is dry, stippling and shading may be recommenced, and the work finished ; or the washing, which produces a soft and beautiful effect, may, if necessary, be renewed at a more advanced stage of the drawing.

ART. 213.—The process of softening off inclined planes is much the same as for cylinders; the difference being a more gradual shade, which will require a little practice in order to avoid the appearance of a curvilinear form when a flat inclined surface is intended to be represented.

COLOURS AND COLOURING.

ART. 214.—The colours used in mechanical drawing being for the most part conventional, it will be sufficient to give a list of what the beginner is likely to require, and how to employ them. The colours and their arrangement may be as follows :—

| Carmine, | Indigo, | Cobalt, | Indian Red, |
| Crimson Lake. | Prussian Blue. | Indian Yellow. | Saturnine Red. |

| Roman Ochre, | Burnt Sienna, | Burnt Umber, |
| Sepia. | Raw Sienna. | Raw Umber. |

With a stick of Indian-ink, Gamboge, and Chinese White.

ART. 215.—*Manipulating with colours.*—The sheet of paper being prepared by washing with clean water (which is essentially necessary if the hands of the draughtsman have been in contact therewith,—see Art. 6), the work may be commenced by washing in all the projected shadows with a light shade of Indian-ink, and afterwards with a deeper tone, to which may be added a slight tinge of the colour representing the material of the objects on which the shadows are cast ; *i.e.,* a little raw sienna for stone, raw umber for wood, and *iron grey* (which we shall presently refer to) for wrought and cast iron. The cast shadows having been washed in, the shading of large cylindrical surfaces (as explained ART. 211.), which require a number of softened washes, should have the first attention ; because

the minor parts of the drawing can be gone on with whilst
the larger parts are drying.

ART. 216.—*Iron grey.*—This is a shade of grey intended to represent the *outer skin* or surface of cast iron,
and is obtained by mixing carmine, or crimson lake, and
indigo with Indian-ink; which colours, from experiments
with the " colour top," we find should be in the proportion
of 1 part carmine to 6 parts of indigo and 27 parts of
Indian-ink. Although these proportions cannot in practice be accurately measured, they will assist the judgment
by showing that the carmine must bear a very small
proportion to the Indian-ink, or the wash of colour will
have a shade of *red*, which ought to be imperceptible;
on the other hand, if blue predominates we shall get a
colour resembling common writing ink, instead of a beautiful iron grey, which, on account of the difficulty of
matching, should be mixed in quantity sufficient for the
whole drawing. When, by evaporation, the colour is quite
dry, a portion for each day's use may be taken from the
edge of the saucer with a damp brush, and the saucer
turned upside down to protect it from dust; and in this
manner it can be kept for weeks.

Cast iron in section, if not shown by section lines, is
represented by a wash of indigo.

Wrought iron in section, if not represented by lines,
receives a tint of Prussian blue.

Either of the above sections may, however, be represented in lines of the respective colours, drawn with the
pen or point of a brush.

The tinting of wrought iron is also in Prussian blue;
the shading being done with Indian-ink and a slight tinge
of iron grey.

Wrought iron and steel polished may have a wash of
cobalt; a line of pure white light being left on the illumined portion of cylindrical surfaces.

Brass.—Shade with burnt umber, wash with Indian
yellow, and tone down, if necessary, with Roman ochre.

Copper will be most satisfactorily represented by Indian red, shading with burnt umber and Roman ochre.

Lead, Tin, or Zinc.—For these materials, indigo with a little Chinese white may be employed.

Wood.—For this material (like stone) a variety of colours may be used; for the groundwork, however, Roman ochre, or raw sienna, grained with burnt sienna, burnt umber, and sepia.

Granite may be represented in the following manner:— Take a number of bristles, such as are used by brush makers, and tie them to the end of a stick; then cut off quite square, and about half an inch long. Take a little indigo in the brush thus made, and having carefully covered with straight or curved strips of paper all the parts of the drawing except that which is to be coloured, hold the brush in the left hand, and with the fore-finger of the right deflect the bristles, so as to throw off small specks of colour upon the uncovered part of the sheet; and the appearance of granite, which may be diversified by using different colours, will be thus obtained.

Brick-work.—Sections of brick-work are invariably represented with a wash of carmine. Brick-work in elevation may be put in with saturnine red, which we have recommended on account of its extreme brilliancy, but which can always be toned down with burnt umber, if desired.

CHAPTER XV.

DRAWING FROM THE MACHINE AND COPYING DRAWINGS.

ART. 217.—The practice of making to scale drawings of actual machines will, to those who have patiently worked out the problems and examples in this book and the Elementary Treatise, now become a very simple matter indeed, and one that will require but few remarks.

The engineer's scale is made in box-wood and in ivory. It is 12 inches long, $1\frac{1}{2}$ inch or $1\frac{1}{4}$ inch wide, and engraved on both sides with scales from $\frac{1}{16}$ of an inch to 1 foot, up to 3 inches. Taking the 1 inch scale as an illustration, the foot is divided into twelve equal parts, each of which is intended to represent 1 foot; that is to say, 1 inch to 1 foot. Again, the first division of the scale being divided into twelve equal parts, each part will represent 1 inch; and so on for all the other scales, from which the measurements are taken with a pair of compasses. There are scales, however, engraved in such a manner that the readings from $\frac{1}{16}$th of an inch to 1 foot, up to 3 inches to 1 foot, can be taken from the two edges of the scale. That is to say, the dimensions of a drawing made to any of the scales from $\frac{1}{16}$th of an inch to 3 inches can be read off by applying the edge of the scale to the lines of which the measurement is required, without the aid of the compasses.

Being provided with a pair of callipers for measuring the diameters of shafts, a plumb line for obtaining their lateral distance when not in the same horizontal plane, and a two-foot rule,—the first thing to be done is to make a careful sketch of the whole or any part of the machine, and proceed to fill in the dimensions, commencing, as a rule, with the ground line and position of main driving

N

shaft, from which dimensions may be taken in every direction; especial regard being paid to the centres of motion, through which horizontal and vertical centre lines should be drawn, and these lines worked from. The dimensions should be carefully marked off thus, $\leftarrow 2'\,4''\frac{9}{16}\rightarrow$

for lateral dimensions, and $\frac{6''\,3}{8}$ for vertical dimensions.

With attention to these remarks and a little *practice*, the best of all instructors, the minor difficulties, if any, will soon disappear, and the result of the first attempt will be, as it invariably has been, a creditable if not a first class drawing from actual measurement.

COPYING DRAWINGS.

ART. 218 —Duplicates of drawings are so frequently required that we deem the various methods which are and have been practised for copying to be deserving of some attention.

Formerly the handles of mathematical drawing pens were made in two parts, and screwed together; to the lower half was attached the pen, and to the upper half a steel point, or pricker, intended to be used in marking off the salient angles and main centres of the drawing to be copied, which was simply fastened down on a plain sheet of paper, and the steel pricker forced through the sheet, so as to leave small punctures on the blank sheet, to serve as guides for putting in the principal centres and main outlines; the minor parts being measured and set off with the compasses. This " pricking off," as it is called, was (after the introduction of tracing paper) superseded by the transfer process.

ART. 219.—*Copying by transfer* is thus performed :— A sheet of black or red transfer paper, which we shall presently describe, is laid with its prepared face upon the sheet of paper on which the drawing is to be copied;

and over this is placed a tracing of the drawing, carefully pinned or weighted down. The right lines of the tracing may now be transferred by going over them with a metallic or other pointed instrument that will not cut the tracing, and in this manner a copy of the original, in red or black lines, afterwards to be inked in, will be obtained. In transferring regular curves or circles, a × will be sufficient to denote the centres, and short lines (1) the radii.

ART. 220.—A sheet of transfer paper, which will last for years, may be thus prepared :—Take half an imperial sheet of very thin paper, similar to that used by hatters, and having strained it upon a board (ART. 3), rub some common black-lead powder well into and all over the sheet; remove the dust and superfluous black-lead; and well rub the sheet with a cotton rag, to prevent its soiling the paper when used for transferring.

Red paper, employed principally by lithographers, is prepared in the same manner, but with red ochre.

ART. 221.—It will be evident from the foregoing explanation that three distinct operations are required by this process to produce a copy of a drawing, namely, *making the tracing, transferring, and drawing the lines in ink;* and yet a drawing can be much more rapidly copied by tracing and transferring, than by measuring off with the compasses or by the old system of pricking off, which few of us remember in practice. Most of us, however, have a recollection of having in our early days copied little pictures by placing them against a pane of glass in the window, than which we can imagine nothing more simple; yet it is only within a few years that this simple and direct mode of copying, with the aid of what may not inappropriately be called a *glass drawing board,* has been adopted in practice.

Imagine a square opening to be cut through a drawing board, leaving a margin, say 3 inches wide, and the edges of the opening to be rebated to receive a sheet of plate glass, let in flush with the face of the board.   This copying or *glass drawing board*, when in use, is placed on a table in front of a window, and supported at an angle of about 25°, so as to get a strong light underneath, which may be further increased by the reflected light from a sheet of white paper laid upon the table.   The original drawing being pinned down on the board, and a sheet of paper (or parchment, if the copy is to be on that material) placed on the top, the work of copying direct with ink may be commenced in the same manner as when making a tracing; and, with a properly adjusted light above the board, the finest lines will be plainly visible.   If the glare óf light on the upper surface is too great, the angle of the board may be increased, or, better still perhaps, the draughtsman's eyes may be protected from the glare by a shade, similar to the peak of a cap, which will render this simple and direct mode of copying both expeditious and satisfactory.

Having explained the chain of our thoughts, as intimated in the preface to the first edition of the Elementary Treatise, we must now leave the student to add, with patience and perseverance, the remaining links.

KELLY & Co., Printers, Gate Street, Lincoln's Inn Fields. W.C.

DRAWING. A.

No 1.

No 2.

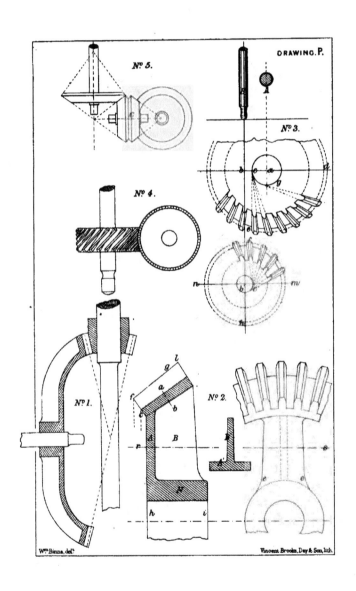

DRAWING. P.

Nº 5.

Nº 3.

Nº 4.

Nº 1.

Nº 2.

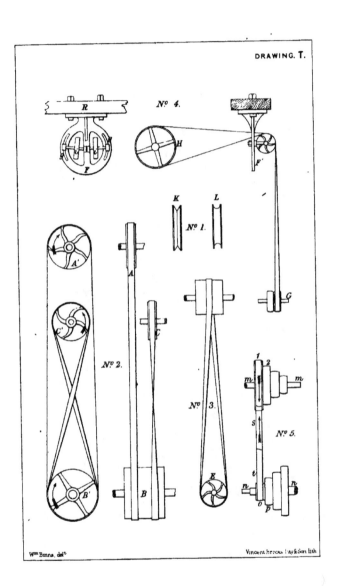

N⁰ 4.

R

H

F'

K   L

N⁰ 1.

A'

A

G

C'

C

N⁰ 2.

N⁰ 3.

1 2

m   m

S

N⁰ 5.

t

n   n

O

B'   B   E   P

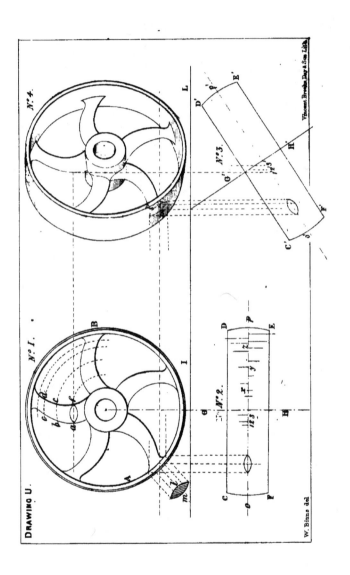

DRAWING U.

N.º 1.

N.º 4.

N.º 2.

N.º 3.

THIS BOOK IS DUE ON THE LAST DATE
STAMPED BELOW

AN INITIAL FINE OF 25 CENTS
WILL BE ASSESSED FOR FAILURE TO RETURN
THIS BOOK ON THE DATE DUE. THE PENALTY
WILL INCREASE TO 50 CENTS ON THE FOURTH
DAY AND TO $1.00 ON THE SEVENTH DAY
OVERDUE.

www.ingramcontent.com/pod-product-compliance
Lightning Source LLC
LaVergne TN
LVHW012203040326
832903LV00003B/101